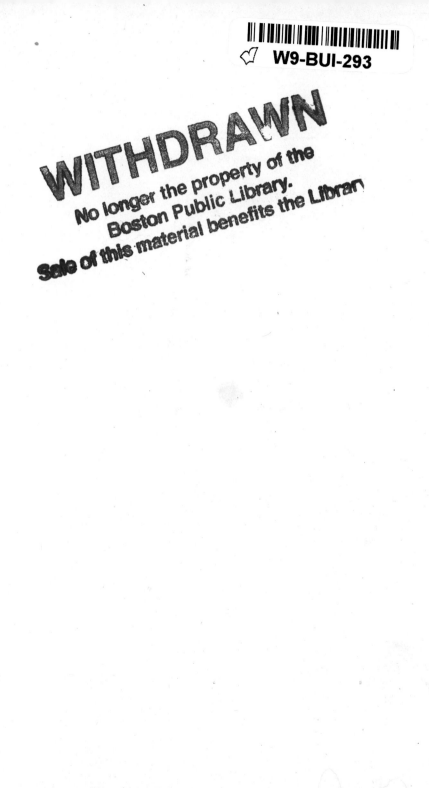

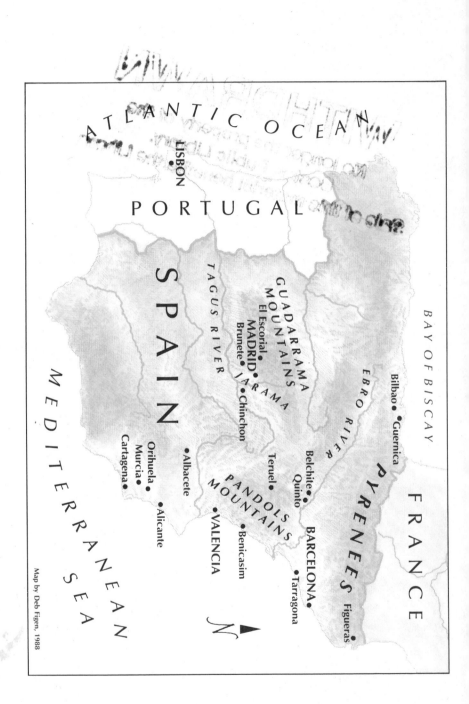

ATLANTIC OCEAN

LISBON

PORTUGAL

SPAIN

TAGUS RIVER

GUADARRAMA MOUNTAINS
El Escorial
MADRID
Brunete
JARAMA
Chinchon

BAY OF BISCAY

Bilbao
Guernica

EBRO RIVER

PYRENEES

FRANCE

MEDITERRANEAN SEA

Orihuela
Murcia
Cartagena

Albacete

Alicante

Teruel

Belchite
Quinto

PANDOLS MOUNTAINS

VALENCIA

Benicasim

BARCELONA

Tarragona

Figueras

N

Map by Deb Figen, 1988

Mississippi to Madrid

Memoir of a Black American
in the Abraham Lincoln Brigade

MISSISSIPPI to MADRID

by JAMES YATES

MEMOIR OF A BLACK AMERICAN IN THE ABRAHAM LINCOLN BRIGADE

OPEN HAND PUBLISHING INC.
Seattle, Washington

Open Hand Publishing Inc.
600 East Pine, Suite 565
Seattle, WA 98122
(206) 323-3868

Photos from the Collection of James Yates
Cover illustration by Selma Waldman
Cover design by Deb Figen

Library of Congress Catalog Card Number: 88-62370

ISBN: 0-940880-19-9 cloth cover
ISBN: 0-940880-20-2 paperback

Printed in the United States of America

95 94 93 92 91 90 89   7 6 5 4 3 2 1

Dedicated to
my daughter Louise
to the memory of my son Richard
to my grandchildren
and great-grandchildren

Table of Contents

	Foreword	
	by John Henrik Clarke	xi
	Preface	xiii
Chapter 1	Surviving Boyhood	15
Chapter 2	Leaving Mississippi	29
Chapter 3	Chicago	43
Chapter 4	Bessie	59
Chapter 5	New York	79
Chapter 6	Leaving for Spain	101
Chapter 7	Spain	113
Chapter 8	Brunete	131
Chapter 9	Going Home	153
Chapter 10	After Spain	163
	Epilogue	173
	Appendix I	175
	Appendix II	176
	Index	178

Foreword

This is a neglected aspect of a larger American story that is both national and international. It is a Black American's story that relates to all Americans and the world struggle of the thirties and the attempts to prevent the spread of fascism and World War II.

The Spanish Civil War and the fight against it did, in part, alert the world to the nature of fascism. The story of the Abraham Lincoln Brigade is generally known. It was a contingent of committed Black and White Americans, three thousand in number, who went to fight against fascism. Had the circumstances been different, some of the Black Americans would have been willing to fight in the Italian-Ethiopian War. Ethiopia was overrun in a matter of months, and there was no organized effort to get Black Americans to fight in this war. Those who were willing to go were left with their frustrations. To some of them fighting with the Abraham Lincoln Brigade in the war against fascism in Spain was an alternative.

In his book, *Mississippi to Madrid: Memoir of a Black American in the Abraham Lincoln Brigade,* James Yates has told the story of the Black Americans who participated in the war with warmth, feeling and dignity. Their original number, from 80 to 100, has now been reduced to 6 or 8 and this is one of the sadder aspects of this story. As these Black Veterans of the Abraham Lincoln Brigade returned to the same racist society they had left, many of them drifted away, some never to be heard from again.

Paul Robeson went to sing for the troops in Spain, and the writer, Langston Hughes, wrote an eye-witness account for Black American newspapers. Angelo Herndon's brother was killed in the fight against Fascism in Spain—but this is only part of the story.

The other part of the story is—what happened to these veterans in the long years after the war was over to the present? How little attention was paid to what they did and why? James Yates's book has uncovered and preserved a little known and yet important episode in Black American History. It belongs in the archives of human struggle.

John Henrik Clarke
Professor African History
Department of African and
Puerto Rican Studies
Hunter College, New York

Preface

In July of 1936 General Francisco Franco led a revolt against the democratically elected government of Spain. Under his command was a well-trained army of mercenaries from Morocco. Italy's Benito Mussolini kept his pledge to Franco by sending one hundred thousand soldiers directly to Spain from the war in Ethiopia. From Germany Adolph Hitler sent artillery, technicians, a large air force and twenty-five thousand tanks. Meanwhile, the Portuguese government dispatched two divisions of soldiers to aid Franco.

These events in Spain stunned and shocked the conscience of people throughout Europe and the world. The government of Spain, in its effort to withstand the attack of the fascist armies, appealed to the democratic governments of the world for their support. Instead of sending help, the governments of England, France and the United States placed an embargo on arms to Spain.

Nevertheless, freedom-loving people from around the world answered Spain's call for help. Within a few months thousands of men and women from many countries flocked to Spain with the hope of stopping fascism. An estimated forty thousand volunteers served in the International Brigades. Of the three thousand from the United States, almost one hundred were Black.

The number of people who fought in the International Brigades was only a small speck when measured against the thousands of Spaniards who fought in the Republican army. However, the role played by the Internationals was very significant in preventing Franco from achieving the quick victory that he expected when his forces attacked Madrid. Madrid held out for three long years.

The war ended in Spain by March, 1939. Poland was invaded by Hitler's Nazi army the following September, thus signaling the start of World War II. What follows here is an account of events that preceded World War II, told from the perspective of one who made that long journey from Mississippi to Madrid.

There have been friends who, directly or indirectly, have helped with the writing of this book. They are too numerous to list. Among them, however, are Doris Nash, Harry Belafonte, Pete Seeger, William Koenig, Jean Fein, William Ford, and especially Janine Hamilton, who helped me in more ways than I have space to tell.

Chapter 1

Surviving Boyhood

One winter day in February of 1937, I found myself on a New York dock boarding a boat—my destination, Spain. There had been many twists and turns that had brought me to this crossroad. There was Chicago and New York. And there were other places . . . but before them all, there was Mississippi, the place where I was born. The year was 1906, that is, if what was written down in the old family bible is correct. There was no other way of knowing, since the state of Mississippi didn't bother to register the birth or death of Black folks.

There in my grandmother's log cabin, my mother Ida Yates, was attended by a midwife. It was in an all-Black community in the bush country. Some call it the sticks, but its true name was the Brown Settlement, named after a farmer plantation owner whose slaves grew corn and cotton.

To the north was Stonewall, a cottonmill town established long before slavery ended. To the south was Quitman, a sawmill town. On the west, miles of lowland along the banks of the Chickasawhay River stretched across gently rolling slopes. To the east was the swiftly flowing Archusa Creek, where I used to play as a boy.

My grandmother Lizzy was fifteen years old when slavery ended. She told me she had just finished washing the breakfast dishes when she heard guns firing. She ran out into the front yard of the white house. Crowding the fence among other slaves, she looked into the distance and saw the Yankees coming. Some of the slaves began to dance openly and shout, but some who were afraid that freedom still wasn't coming just watched the Yankees in awed silence. The slavemaster, having retreated from the battlefields, returned home a few days earlier and hid some of his cows and pigs and other valuables in the swamp. He took his gun and marched a large number of field slaves into the swamp too. That was where he was now hiding, still hoping that the war would turn out like he wanted and slavery would go right on as it had before.

The Yankees came up the road in their dusty blue uniforms and by then nearly every slave in the yard was grinning and shouting, and one even brought out his banjo and began to play. A Yankee officer wanted to know the whereabouts of the slaveowner and the livestock and other things that had been stripped from the big house.

The answer pounded in Grandma's chest louder than the guns that had been firing, but fear still kept her lips sealed. By the time she managed to overcome her fear, a young field slave had already said defiantly, "In the swamp. Mean ol' scamp is hid out yonder in the swamp. Got pigs and cows. Got my daddy, too."

"As the Lord is my witness," Grandma said to me, "boy, you can't know the shame I had been feeling all these years 'cause I wasn't the first to tell that Yankee officer what he wanted to know. Stood there under that hot sun like a worm too scared to crawl. Don't care if your mama is so anxious to keep you alive she'd train you to the contrary, I sure hope nobody ever shut your mouth up like that."

As a free people, Grandmother and the other former slaves continued to work from sunup to sundown, but now they were paid fifty cents a day. This didn't last long though. With the help of the sharecropping and commissary systems, and the fear inspired by the Ku Klux Klan, the former slaveowners regained control over their properties.

My father's name was George Washington Yates, but he was known as "Gipson". He was born in the State of Alabama, but like other ex-slaves, his family drifted all over the country in search of this thing called "freedom." The family wandered as far north as the State of Kansas. Thousands of other ex-slaves went too, many of whom died from the severe cold, despite the help of the friendly people of Kansas. My grandfather decided to move to a warmer climate. This was after my father and my uncle John had gone to school and learned to read and write.

On their way south my family stopped off at Stonewall, the cotton milltown. It was here that my mother and father met and were married. Another part of the family, Dad's sister and my uncle, couldn't take living in Mississippi and went west to Bola, Oklahoma, an all-Black town. I remember one of his letters to my daddy saying he had joined the Marcus Garvey movement. He was waiting, he said, for a ship to take him and others back to Africa.

There were three of us children: my big sister Idella, my little sister Annie, and myself. My father wasn't just a cotton picker or corn puller. He was a jack-of-all-trades. "Learned my trade by not being lazy, boy," he would say to me. "I'd be working under a white man as his helper, but the more they piled work on me, the more I learned. Pretty soon they'd just go sit in the shade and leave me out there working in the sun. When you go lazybones like that, you get rusty. I ended up knowing more about the trade than they did."

In 1912, I was about six years old and ready to begin school, but there were no schools for Black children in the vicinity. Mama and Papa got together with some other folks and they pooled what little money they had and hired a private teacher, someone who had the equivalent of a seventh grade education. Our school was set up in the church. Tuition was fifty cents a month. Unfortunately, even at this low rate, most of the time the people still couldn't afford to pay the teacher, so the plan didn't work out.

My folks were determined that I get some kind of education. I ended up walking ten miles to Brown's Settlement to attend the same log cabin school that my grandmother and mother had once attended. I was taught by the same school teacher, Mr. Thomas Blakeney. In the evening I traveled another ten miles to get back home.

The school, which consisted of some old wooden benches and beat up desks crammed into a small room, was dominated by an old pot-bellied wood-burning stove. It was allowed to remain open only five months out of the year. The other months were cotton chopping, cotton picking or pulling and corn shucking time, or time set aside for other chores that the big landowner might need us for. The governor, the mayors and the sheriffs of the counties kept a close watch on us and saw to it that all Black schools were closed so that our labor would be available to the owners of the land.

My mother, who I mentioned had attended this school, described how it was in her day. "We young ex-slaves were all in this room together. When we couldn't squeeze into the room, classes were conducted in shifts. Those who had to wait their turn sat by the creek or waded in the cool, running water, catching tadpoles, watching the fish, or hunting for four-leafed clovers, or chased butterflies."

Things hadn't changed much since then. There was still the same schoolhouse and the same teacher. We played in the same creek. One thing new was added— baseball, with balls made from rags, and broomsticks used as bats.

While we played Professor Blakeney's voice would ring out, "Get on in here, you scamps, and get some education into your heads!" We quit clowning around and went into the classroom immediately. Professor Blakeney was not to be messed with.

From behind his old scarred desk, he peered at us over his spectacles. He must have been at least eighty years old and could have been a hundred, but he still moved about like a man half that age. He rode a mule to school. Sometimes we'd try to out-race him, taking shortcuts through the bush, traveling along narrow cowpaths, while he rode his mule along the open dirt road. But no matter how fast we ran, he'd be there outside the schoolhouse door mounted on the mule frowning down at us, as we collapsed panting and sweating upon the ground.

Professor Blakeney had been taught to read by his slavemaster's wife, who had eluded her husband and secretly taught the young boy how to read and write. In spite of breaking the law, Blakeney developed a passion for books. Folks said he would go out and sit under a tree and read by moonlight when he didn't have kerosene to burn in his lamp. We were all just a little afraid of Professor Blakeney and some of us thought him outright nutty. His eyes burned at us and not only did he say things we didn't understand but things we almost didn't dare to relate to.

"In less than one hundred years," he said one day, with so much conviction I wanted to look over my shoulder to see if the sheriff was listening, "we will have a Black President of the United States of America! A great day is coming when Blacks will be voting all over Mississippi! The Blacks and poor whites are going to get together and vote their own people into government. That's right! Mark my words. Get prepared. I don't want to hear any more complaints out of you when I say study!"

We couldn't help laughing at him. How could we think of a Black man as president, when all we saw of Blacks was in the fields or in the white folks' kitchen, or as an occasional tradesman getting low pay like my father? Some of the boys kept on playing while the Professor talked.

Later, outside the schoolhouse, Strawberry wrestled June Bug to the ground and smeared mud on his face. His high pitched voice shook with laughter and humor. "I elects this blackest of Black boys as the next number one president of d'ese here New'Nited States," he said while still smearing the mud. Frank and I laughed so hard our stomachs ached.

On the issue of voting, no one acted as crazy about it as the Professor. He'd get on his mule and ride all the way to Meridian and try to vote. The white folks told him not to come back. But every election year he was back on his mule, making a twenty-five mile trip, each way, to cast his ballot. A few years before he died some people worked him over good at the polling place . . . he was never really well again.

There was a mass lynching near the town of Shubuta where the highway and railroad cross the Chickasawhay River. Some parts of the incident were written up in the northern newspapers. No one was ever charged with the crime, although the local members of the Ku Klux Klan were well known. Five men and four women were hung, their feet dangling just inches above the river's muddy waters. Such was Mississippi in those times. The only thing a Black man or woman had to do to get lynched was not move off the sidewalk for "Miss Ann" or "Mr. Charlie." A Black must never be caught drinking from a "White Only" fountain, or making the mistake of using the front door instead of the back door. Stealing a chicken or a pig was very dangerous. Being caught at this could get you twenty years on the chain gang. If you were Black in Mississippi, lightning would surely strike home sooner or later. Here's an example of how it struck in Quitman:

Around 1918 my Uncle Willie, while working in the sawmill one day, accidentally hit a white man with a piece of lumber he was carrying. He managed to make it home after being chased away from the mill. The news spread like wildfire all through town. Password, "Lynching tonight!"

I can remember Grandma Lizzie pacing the floor all through the afternoon. Aunt Belle, my uncle's wife, was almost speechless. He would die fighting rather than be hung by the Kluxers. The only problem now was a supply of ammunition. That day the town merchants had stopped selling shells to Black folks.

Living almost next door to my Uncle Willie was a white family, the Lennons: a husband, a wife and three daughters. We called the man "Mr. Gus." He had an unusual way of speaking English. I could only catch one or two words out of ten. Mr. Gus knew more about lumber than anybody at the sawmill in Quitman. Still, he was an outcast, "white trash" to most white people. It was said he came from up North, but I often heard him talk about Ireland, a place I never heard about before.

Mr. Gus was small in structure but big in heart. He'd heard the news that the Ku Klux Klan was going to lynch my uncle that night. Uncle Willie heard a voice coming from the wooded area, just to the rear of his house. "Willie! Willie!" Mr. Gus wanted to be sure my uncle wouldn't start shooting. Mr. Gus asked my uncle, "What can I do to help you?"

Uncle Willie told him about how the white merchants even refused to sell rabbit-shot to Blacks. Mr. Gus walked away without saying a word. He made his way to Quitman and bought ammunition, then returned to my uncle's house with it. "Here," he said, "defend yourself." Then he went back to town and told the whites, "Some of you will get killed by those niggers if you try to lynch that Willie."

As darkness approached, things got tense. Grandma had fainted and had to be dragged to the chicken coop where she and Aunt Belle would spend the night. By this time, Papa was struggling with Mama who was trying to stop him from joining Uncle Willie and the other two men who vowed to make a stand. As Papa rushed out of the house with his gun, Mama, my two sisters and I made our way to the big rosebush in the back yard. It was a dark night. The skies glittered with twinkling stars. Everything became very quiet, except for the hoot owls and the singing frogs. Mama kept whispering, "Oh my Lord, save us!"

My little sister would now and then let out a groan from the thorny rosebush, but I was quiet as a church mouse. I was thinking about how close our house was to the highway, and I pictured trucks filled with hostile Kluxers. That was one of the longest nights I ever endured, and a thorny rosebush was our bed.

When the first rooster crowed, we knew daylight wasn't far away. Mama calmed down from her praying. I said, "Mama, you say the Lord loves everybody. Why does he let white folks treat us Blacks like this?" Her answers were never good enough for me. I lay there, still searching for the "whys."

Then I asked, "Mama, why didn't the Lord create some Black angels? In all the Sunday School books and the bible all you see are white folks." Mama replied, "Boy . . ." Whenever Mama came out with "boy!" I knew to stop whatever I was doing or saying. She finished . . . "Stop questioning the Lord's will."

About this time we heard voices coming from the wooded area just behind Uncle's house. We saw Papa, Uncle Willie, Mr. Hub and Mr. Joe coming out with their guns. Grandmama Lizzie and Aunt Belle came out of the chicken coop at the same time. Aunt Belle, wanting to celebrate the fact that we were all alive, made a hot breakfast for everyone. It was like Freedom Day again for Grandmama, and she was dancing all over the house.

It was about this time that I quit school. It seemed useless somehow to keep on going. At best, I would end up with a third-rate education, qualifying me for only the worst kinds of jobs, that is, if I didn't cross the wrong white man at the wrong time and get myself killed. After the incidents at Shubuta I had only one obsession. That was to get up North to magic places like Chicago and New York, where I'd heard there was some freedom, and where white folks didn't shoot you, lynch you, and insult you every day. Most of the young fellows I knew felt the same way. We picked and chopped cotton and fed the hogs and cows, and dreamed of that wonderful day when we'd head North.

I was about thirteen when I looked for work and found a job at a brickyard. I hauled bricks in a wheelbarrow that was so heavy it felt like it would snatch off my arms. I stacked bricks and acted as the general helper to the white workmen. When there was no work in the fields, I worked at the yard six days a week, twelve hours a day, for fifty cents a day. Up before daybreak in the mornings, Mama made me a hot breakfast, prepared my lunch basket, and a hot supper when I came home in the evening. My skinny arms felt like they were going to break off. Still, I didn't seem to be working half as hard Mama was. She cooked for us, went to the fields with Papa, tended her little garden in the back of the house, which had tomatoes, snap beans, sweet potatoes, collard and turnip greens, all of which kept us from going hungry from time to time. Papa also worked at every job he could find. It seemed like the minute we opened our eyes and began the day, we were working and working but we never appeared to be getting anywhere.

I remember my first payday at the brickyard. On Saturday everyone got paid three dollars, or so I thought. I'd give Mama and Papa two dollars for household expenses and keep one dollar for my fare North. After the white workers got paid, the Black workers stood in line. We were outside on the porch of the company store. The boss sat behind a table he'd rigged up and each worker passed before him and got paid off. I stuck out my hand, anticipating the feel of those precious three dollars.

The boss put a voucher in my hand. Marked on it was, "Worth three dollars in the company store." In the company store things were twice as high as in the regular stores. Before I could catch my tongue, I blurted out, "Mr. Gibbs, I don't want no voucher. I want my real money."

One would have thought I had just thrown a stick of dynamite, the way everybody turned and stared at me. Black folks dropped their eyes, cleared their throats and moved back a little. Even my buddy, Elijah, quit talking to the man who stood in line in front of him and just stood there as if he had been stung by a bumblebee.

The boss, Mr. Gibbs, simply looked up at me out of his chinaberry-colored eyes. He drank from a bottle of Dr. Pepper. A drop from the bottle escaped from his thin lips and stained his white shirt. He didn't raise his voice at me yet, but he spoke loud enough so that everyone around would be sure to hear. "What you say again, boy? You don't like our store here, you say?"

I guess I was crazy to keep on talking. "Naw suh," I said. "I mean, yassuh. I loves your store. But just to get a stick of candy your prices run twice as high as anywhere else . . ." I couldn't make my voice go on. All the other white men had stopped what they were doing now and were taking another look at me.

Mr. Tatum had opened the screen door and stepped onto the porch to watch us. The men at the checkerboard had swung their faces in my direction. Mr. Skeeter, the cracker who, it was said, had thrown Strawberry's mama down and took her, didn't look up from the straw hat tilted over his face. Still I knew his eyes were on me. As for the white men I worked with, some had already gone home, but three of them, including Mr. Joe, hadn't. Mr. Joe had one foot lifted to climb aboard his wagon where his wife, Miss Luella, and his brood of children sat. His other foot seemed unable to follow and he hung there almost like he was trying to lift the wagon up off the road, his face twisted around towards us. The other workers just stood there near the porch, pretending they were suddenly interested in the old bulldog lying there upon the tobacco juice-spattered grounds, its pink tongue puffing in and out against the evening heat, its ears and tail beating away flies.

"By gum," Mr. Gibbs said, "Y'all ever heard of such a thing?" He looked around at Mr. Tatum and Mr. Skeeter and Mr. Gumption, all of whom also wore white shirts. Then he looked out at Mr. Joe and the other two men transfixed over the dog. "Boy here complaining about our store. White folks buy at the store and I ain't heard no complaints. Yet this boy is running off at the tongue like he's somebody special."

"Who's boy is he?" Tatum wanted to know.

"I don't know him," Mr. Gibbs said. "You from around here?" "Quitman, suh," I said. "I . . . I . . ." "I know his folks," Mr. Gumption said. "Good law-abiding folks. Never no sass—hard workers." Mr. Gibbs pushed aside his Dr. Pepper and looked at Mr. Gumption. "If they such good folks, how come they ain't taught this boy some sense? If it ain't sass he's standing right before my face and chucking at me, what is it?" "I expect he's a good boy," Mr. Gumption defended. "Sun been powerfully hot all day. Anybody liable to get a little sunstroke."

"Here, boy," Mr. Gibbs said. "Now you take this voucher and go on a-home, less you want to spend it now. And next time you try to keep a little watch on your uppity ways."

I hesitated. All the air seemed to be sucked out of the day. Maybe I did have a sunstroke of some kind. I noticed Mr. Skeeter, his straw hat tilted rakishly to one side. He walked over lazily. Black folks said Mr. Skeeter had trouble sleeping nights if he hadn't whipped himself one or two niggers during the day.

"You deaf?" Mr. Skeeter said. "You didn't hear Mr. Gibbs? Nigger, I been seeing you looking for somebody to sass. Now, do you want to sass me?" Shame flooded me, as

I knew I was going to reach out and accept the voucher Mr. Gibbs held in his hand.

"Nawsuh," I said.

"Then grab that voucher and get your Black ass out of here."

I took the voucher and turned to go. Mr. Skeeter raised his foot and kicked me as hard as he could in the rear. I went sailing off the porch and my face landed in the dust. Green flies winged past my eyes. A smell so filthy stung my nostrils that I almost vomited.

Elijah helped me up and wiped my face. He put his arm around my shoulder and walked me home. His big body shook as though he had a spasm, and I couldn't stop myself from crying.

We slipped past my two sisters playing hopscotch with some youngsters out in front and found Mama in the back-yard. She wore a sunbonnet and chopped vigorously at the weeds in her garden. She took one look at my face and missed a lick with the hoe. The blade sliced a tomato bush and the stalk bent toward the earth.

"Boy, what on earth? Elijah, what happened?" Alarm and fear clawed at the serenity that she sometimes man-aged to seal over her face. Between my choked-up efforts to tell her, and Elijah hotly and angrily explaining to her, she understood.

She was speechless for a moment. Then her eyes took on a wildness as she said, "Lord have mercy! But Jesus God, don't tell your daddy, son. Don't tell him a single word. Lord, I been praying these crackers wouldn't load no extra straw on your daddy's back. Elijah, tell all the folks who seen it to just hush up and don't tell him noth-ing. Sure as the sun rises, the way he loves this boy, he'll go after that Skeeter cracker and his life wouldn't be worth a Confederate nickel!"

She had her arm around me and tried to clean away what was left of the mess on my face with her work-roughed hands. Elijah left and she went into the house and got a pan of water and some soap and washed the smell away.

She looked up at the late evening sky. Her voice trembled and her small shoulders shook as she said, "One of these days, son, the good Lord ain't going to send down nothing but fire and brimstone, and every no-good cracker on this earth is going to burn to cinders! Just you wait and see, boy. God ain't blind to all this evil down here."

I looked up at the motionless white clouds, and I loved her and wanted to believe her, but sometimes I had a few doubts about what she spied in the sky.

■ ■ ■

The Bilbo family's roots go far back in the history of Mississippi. With the end of slavery, they emerged on the political scene as the strong arm of the plantation owners. Theodore Gilmore Bilbo moved up the ladder in political circles and became a United States Senator from the State of Mississippi. He became notorious in his filibustering against any bill in the Senate which could make life better for the millions of Blacks who lived in the South. Thousands of Blacks left the plantations and migrated north hoping for a better life. When the southern establishment could not keep the Blacks down on the farm, their political arm in Congress, Senator Bilbo, proposed that we deport sixteen million Blacks back to Africa.

I lived in a state ruled by Bilbo and by Ku Klux Klanners, who committed against Black people some of the most vicious acts imaginable. During my last five years in Mississippi, 1917 to 1922, more than fifty Blacks were lynched. This number would be doubled if the great waters of the Mississippi River could reveal the bodies hidden there. I was a witness to some of these lynchings. Thousands of Black men escaped being lynched but were given life sentences on the Mississippi chain gang. They died a slow death of torture, due to people like Bilbo.

Black soldiers returning home from World War I were imprisoned for disobeying orders by not discarding their uniforms within the three-day limit set by the local authorities.

One week after quitting the brickyard, I was hired at a sawmill in Quitman. My job was to haul lumber on a two-wheeled cart. But this time it was a mule pushing and tugging the load instead of me. At the sawmill I was paid one dollar for a ten hour day, as compared to the twelve hour day at the brickyard. Although things were a little better, in a way it was too little too late.

All my thoughts began to turn to the time I would be on my way North. I gave myself a year, spring of 1923, at the latest, and I began counting the months. Money or no money, I was ready to take a chance.

Chapter 2

Leaving Mississippi

The slaves called the North "up-south." In the early nineteen twenties, a half million Blacks were on their journey up-south, to Chicago, St. Louis, Detroit, while others made their way west as far as California. "Going North" was made famous by Black composer W.C. Handy. The blues were being made popular by the great Louis Armstrong blowing his horn, "I Got the St. Louis Blues." Bessie Smith sang, "I'm Going to Chicago," "I Got the Crazy Blues," "I Got the Jail House Blues." For those who wanted to stop off at the building of the Alabama Muscle Shoals Dam, there was "I Got the Muscle Shoals Blues." Bessie Smith was badly wounded in an auto accident in Alabama and died because she was refused emergency care at an all-white hospital.

One Saturday morning in 1923 while Mama was making a hot breakfast as usual, I got dressed with all my going-away clothes on under my work overalls. Mama said, "Boy! You look mighty fat this morning." "Oh, Mama, you're seeing things again," I answered, turning and walking away without saying goodbye. It was the only way I could leave that morning.

Instead of going to work, I met my two buddies, Frank Moody and Elijah Collins, down beside the riverbank. We stayed there until pay time. We worried that the white boss might be waiting at the pay office to find out why we didn't come to work that day. We were lucky. He wasn't there. We collected our six dollars, all the money we had to take us north. I was sixteen years old.

We avoided the highway to keep out of sight of the white folks, and walked ten miles through the swamps. We came out of Alligator Swamp at the railroad trestle, where the tracks crossed a small body of water that flows into the Chickasawhay River. To the east, we heard the barking of dogs from Brown Settlement. From just across the river came the sound of drums from the Indian reservation. Frank Moody said, "We got five miles to go before we reach Stonewall."

We shrugged, wondering which one of us would be the bravest and act as "travel agent" and go buy the tickets? Elijah, being the tallest and having a deep voice like a man, volunteered.

With tickets in our hands, we heard a whistle blow. This was the train to Meridian, where we would change for one going to Birmingham, Alabama. We'd all made a pact to make our leaving home a secret. As the train pulled into Stonewall Station, I heard a scuffling behind me. It was Elijah's daddy. I knew then that something had gone wrong. One of us had talked. Elijah's Daddy had no time to grab Frank and me. We had already slipped onto the train.

When Frank and I finally reached Meridian, the second largest city in the state, we pondered our next step. Had the police been notified to pick us up? We entered the dingy little waiting room labeled "Blacks Only." There we blended in with the other children and their parents.

The train moved slowly out of the station on its way to Birmingham. "Just two more youngsters under age," the conductor must have thought, as he walked past us without a glance. We were in a segregated coach behind the engine. There were only a few seats. The rest of the coach was reserved for the mail. The mailman, of course, was

Black, as the smoke-filled car was considered too dangerous for whites.

Early next morning, a few minutes past seven, we
arrived in Birmingham, Alabama. My friend Frank had the
address of a rooming house. We wandered around this big
station, being sure to avoid the white folks's waiting room.
Soon we found a door leading to the street. Waiting there
was a coach taxi yoked to a big white horse. We asked the
taxi driver how much it would cost to take us to the
rooming house. "Fifty cents," he said. Off we went, riding
behind the horse at a slow trot. If I remember clearly, he
took us down Eighteenth Street. There the taxi-man called
out, "Whoa! Whoa!" The horse came to a halt in front of a
two-story frame house. He said, "Boys, we are here!"

We paid our bill. I rang the bell. A rather pleasant
woman in her late fifties answered the ring. Frank asked
her if she had a room. In a soft voice she said, "I sure do,
boys. Come on in."

It seemed like a perfect place to stay. A big window
overlooked the street. Frank took in the view of the big
city. He called out to me, "Jimmy, come and look at what I
see!" I ran over to the window. "What?" The railroad station
from where we'd taken the taxi a short while before was
just across the street. "Boy," I said to Frank, "we have been
taken for a ride!" Instead of telling us the house was half a
block from the station, the taxi driver drove us around a
long circle and dropped us off where we almost began.

The woman of the house wanted to know where we
were from. We told her, "Mississippi, ma'am!" "Boys," she
said, "you know around here there is all kinds of danger.
The white folks will pick you up if they catch you loafing
around in the street. They say they are hiring men to work
in the mine out in Ansley." This was a little town about
thirty-five miles from Birmingham.

The next day was a Monday. Frank and I were on the
way to the mine shaft. It was a three mile walk. When we
reached there, we saw a long line of men waiting near the

mine shaft to be hired for the night shift. Frank and I joined them. Long after midday we were hired.

I looked at Frank. He seemed frightened. I wondered if he was thinking the same thing I was, about digging coal one or two miles underground! At that moment, the day shift came out from the pit. They were dressed in white from head to foot, looking like the Ku Kluxers back in Mississippi. I turned to Frank. "Boy, this is not a coal mine. Have you ever seen white coal? Let's get out of here!" It took us only a short time to get back to Ansley from where we caught the train back to Birmingham.

Frank didn't even want to stay in Birmingham. We wandered across the street to the railroad station. No sooner had we entered the waiting room for Blacks than a white man, standing in the doorway, called to Frank, "Boy, come here!"

We wondered what was up now. What had we done wrong? A white man wanted to see us! "Boy," he told Frank, "I got work for you, if you want to go up to Kentucky working on the railroad."

Frank asked him, "Mister, what about my younger brother?"

"Oh, he's too young," the white man said.

"Mister," said Frank, "the only way I go is with my brother."

While I held my breath, the white man said, "O.K. He can come along. We'll be leaving at midnight. Meet me at Gate nine."

At a few minutes after midnight the train pulled out of the station. We were the two most happy boys in the world, still traveling north on our way to Chicago. We had no idea what this railroad job would be like, but we were getting a free ride, paid for by the railroad. Still, I wondered why the conductor said at every stop, "Boys, pull down your window shades."

We found out why when we entered the State of Kentucky. As the train pulled to a stop in a small town, one of the Blacks decided to raise his shades for a little peep out, and this brought a hail of stones toward our coach. Now we understood why we were asked to pull down the shades. No Blacks were allowed in this town.

At nine in the morning, the train pulled over to a side track. Our two coaches were uncoupled, while the rest of the train went on its way north. Standing on our side of the track were three other cars, two for sleeping and one for eating. We were given a big breakfast, and the tall lanky white man who had come all the way from Birmingham with us called, "Boys! Out on the track!"

As I was the youngest, the boss called to me, "Boy! Take this flag and go with this man. He'll show you where to stand and wave all the trains down to a stop."

Frank was as big and strong as an ox. He could work as long as the older men, laying rail. The blazing sun was like what it was at home in the cotton fields. By two o'clock, men began to pass out from the heat. By the time we stopped for lunch, those who could, crawled to the table and ate. Others were so fatigued, they just laid around on the floor.

Frank sat at my right, on the end of the old wooden bench. I could easily whisper to him without being overheard. Our whole conversation was about what to do next. We glanced out the door of the coach. All woods. And what about that huge black monster of a dog? I noticed Frank stuffing bones in his pockets.

I asked him, "Frank, what are we going to do?"

"Get your little sack over near the door as soon as we're finished eating," he replied.

On the doorstep, we sat observing the dog. Now and then Frank would throw him some scraps. He said, "I think he's becoming more friendly." I could not see any change and thought, what if another vicious hound was waiting to pounce on us as soon as we made for those swampy woods? Frank pulled a big bone from his pocket and threw it to the dog. It was the perfect time to make our getaway. Frank said, "Now's our chance. Let's make for the woods!"

We started walking. We figured if we made a wide enough circle, we'd come out of the swamp at a point far beyond where the men might be looking for us. We found a spring where the water wasn't too dirty, and drank and washed up. We spied a patch of blackberries and began eating them, but within seconds we heard rattling. One of the biggest rattlesnakes I'd ever seen guarded the patch. I led Frank away from the bush and we kept moving.

Hours later, with the sun slowly dying, we broke through a clearing and saw a small town ahead of us. We couldn't restrain our relief. We broke into grins even though we wondered how it would be possible to find where the Blacks lived who would give us food without running across whites who would start asking questions. We made our way cautiously toward the town, jumping behind trees so as not to be seen. There was one main street with a general store and several smaller streets that spread out from the center. At the edge of town, we saw a water tower, the kind from which the engines of trains were filled. Though we couldn't see the tracks yet, we knew the railroad must be over there somewhere. "Once we get something to eat," I said, "we can go on a little piece out of town, grab the next freight train and be long gone!"

Frank nodded and looked out over the town uneasily. We were in Pine Knot, Kentucky. A few white people had seen us, but they only turned around, stared at us sharply, then went on. A lot of them were standing around the general store in front of a building marked "Saloon," from which music could be heard. Those who were not standing sat in cane-bottomed chairs leaning back against the whitewashed walls, hats pulled over their eyes. Frank and I ducked behind a building and vainly looked for a Black face. Where would they be? Out there beyond the edge of town, across the railroad tracks?

We started into the street again. Then Frank jumped back, with his eyes bulging out of his head. He pointed to a banner that hung across the street. We could both read well enough to make out the bold crude letters: "No Niggers Allowed in this Town." We stared at the sign and turned and ran like hell. We expected any minute to hear guns being shot at us by the men near the saloon and the general store. But maybe we had caught them by surprise and they didn't have time to get guns. We heard nothing behind us except the yelping of a dog. We didn't stop running until we were a long way from that town.

We didn't go very far back into the swamp. We tried to keep parallel to where we thought the railroad tracks might be. In time we curved toward it, still running, then continued along the tracks themselves until we found a hilly place where the train would be climbing at a slower speed. We would try to catch it there. We flopped down into a ditch at the edge of the embankment and prepared to wait. We thought our wait would be a matter of a few hours. Nearly ten hours passed. Hungry and dispirited, we heard a freight chugging towards us in the distance.

We didn't know anything about hoboing except what we had heard from older men. You catch the train going uphill at its slowest speed. You keep a sharp lookout for railroad detectives, be careful not to fall and land under the wheels, and get into an empty boxcar if you can find one.

We allowed the engine and a few cars to go past before jumping out of our hiding place and running to hop the freight. It chugged up the incline faster than we had expected.

Frank stumbled on a cross tie and almost fell while I veered around to avoid tripping over him. He managed to stay on his feet. I grabbed for the iron rungs on a boxcar, hoping that Frank would be able to catch the same car. Nearly all of my breath was snatched out of me, but I hung on. I saw Frank running and straining to catch up. He missed the car I clung to, but caught the one directly behind.

Slowly I climbed to the top of the car. Then I began crawling back to the car where Frank was. I wished we'd been able to get inside of a boxcar. Now we'd have to ride on top or hold onto the side of the train. It could be freezing cold outside.

The train swayed beneath me. I crawled carefully, painfully aware of the spinning earth, and of the deep drop-off on either side of the train. I had managed to inch half the distance to Frank's car, when I sensed someone behind me. I gripped the car and turned my head. A pair of brown brogan shoes were coming towards me. Their owner was treading the car like he was walking in the streets. When I got a glimpse of the man's unfriendly face and the black billy club that he held in his right hand, I knew he was a railroad detective, hired to throw hobos off the train. He stood over me. I clung to the quaking train, feeling totally helpless. What could I do? How could I escape being clubbed even if I tried? But he did nothing. Just stood over me. Either he was enjoying my helplessness or had decided to let me go. The train swayed violently and I lost my grip. I couldn't break the fall. In a moment I'd go over the side of the car. I was vaguely aware that the man could arrest my fall if he wanted to. Desperately my fingers clawed at the car, seeking a grip. Just when my mind had given up and I began to anticipate the impact from the fall, I caught onto the rough edges at the top of the car. I hung on with my fingertips, suspended over the ground speeding away below. I gazed up pleadingly into the man's face. He looked as tall as the sun. He had a big red nose speckled by dark hairy moles. Around his neck hung a blue bandanna, as blue as his eyes. All the while I had been falling, I don't think he even moved. Now he squatted and looked me in the face. Tears gushed from my eyes. Silently I begged him for help. I couldn't have pleaded harder if I had been looking up at God. There was no particular expression on his face. At most, he seemed curious as to how long I would be able to hold onto the car. He slapped the club into the palm of his hand and waited for me to fall. Finally he frowned in annoyance that I didn't hurry up and drop from sight. He lifted the club and slammed it near my fingers. When I still didn't let go, the next lick came down upon my knuckles and I saw red and blue stars. I lost my grip and tumbled toward the earth.

The swampy ground softened my fall. Blindly I rolled away from the cross ties and the grinding of the train. My left leg had caved under me, and I thought I had actually heard the snap of one of my fingers as it broke. Still, I crawled to my feet almost immediately. Fear of spending the night alone in the swamp propelled me back up the embankment. I hobbled alongside the speeding train. But soon I knew I'd never be able to reboard it. The boxcars sailed past me with an alarming swiftness. And with each step I took, my leg shot a painful brightness into my brain. Still I ran, if you could call it that, hoping I could stay on my feet long enough to reach out and grab a car and be snatched aboard. Nearly all the cars had passed when someone yelled, "Here, boy, here!" As a boxcar came abreast I saw a grey-haired white man holding out his hand and reaching for me. I was so surprised by a white hand being extended to aid me, I almost didn't reach back. Another detective? Maybe once I was inside he would amuse himself by beating me. If I had time to think I would have refused the hand. But now I felt it grasp mine. "Jump!" And I jumped and was jerked and pulled into the car.

I lay there with the breath heaving from my chest waiting to be struck. Nothing happened. Maybe the man sensed that. No matter what happened, I intended to try and fight back this time, and he would just have to kill me to get me off the train. When there was still no move toward me, I looked around. The man no longer paid any attention to me. He sat near the door and between his knees he nursed a bottle of red wine. From time to time, he took a large swallow. Though his hair was greasy, matted and dirty, he didn't seem as old as he had at first. There was a blank red socket where one of his eyes should have been. "Leg broke?" he suddenly asked.

"Suh?"

"Your leg broke?"

"I don't know, suh."

He sat his bottle down carefully. He pushed himself from the wall and crawled over to me, wobbling with the train. He seemed to be more sober than I thought. With experienced fingers he touched my foot, my ankle, my knee, then suddenly gave the leg a sharp pull and I nearly screamed.

"No. Not broke. Sprung maybe. You ought to be all right now."

I didn't say anything. After a short time, my leg actually felt better, but my finger hurt badly. I clutched it with my hand and didn't let him see it. Not that I doubted he would help with it, but I couldn't get over how he had already helped me. He went back to his place near the door and lifted the wine to his lips again. "Where are you going?"

"Suh?"

"Where you trying to git to?"

"Covington, Kentucky." I still didn't dare say Chicago. Say that to a white man and even if he was disposed to being friendly, his attitude might change. Uppity niggers, going to Chicago.

The man gazed at his bottle. He didn't seem to be talking to anyone in particular.

"Work in a sawmill, join a union," he said. "Work in a steel mill, join a union. Work shoveling shit, join yourself a union."

"Yassuh," I said carefully. I wondered if he wasn't a bit crazy, like Professor Blakeney.

"If they knock out your eyes, break your legs, try and starve you to death, don't fink, come right back in there with a union."

"Yassuh," I said.

And then he was silent.

He said nothing more until we came to Covington, Kentucky. Then it was only to arouse himself and say good-bye.

At the station, Frank came running up to me. He had evaded the detective, jumped off the train, waited awhile and then got on again. He had not been able to crawl inside a boxcar so he rode the freight by clinging to the outside. At some point he tore his overalls and his knee poked out of the hole every time he took a step.

His big eyes regarded me anxiously. "You all right?"

"Just my finger," I said. "I think it's broke."

His eyes shifted with guilt. "By God, if I'd had a six-by-four or a gun, I would've nailed that cracker when I saw him after you! But I didn't have nothing . . ."

"I'm all right," I said. "Just my finger . . ." It hurt so bad, I thought I was going to faint. There was nothing Frank could have done to help me get away from the detective even if he had been brave enough or crazy enough to try. He would have just gotten killed. Still, for a moment, as we entered the station, ashamed of our helplessness, our eyes avoided each other.

We remained in the station and found the toilet with the sign "Colored" over it. From a trash can Frank came up with a piece of wood and he broke it, measuring it against my finger as a splint. He told me to pull the finger hard before he wrapped it, so that the bone would come back into place. I tried it. But he became so disturbed seeing me in such pain that he looked like he was going to faint before I did. He tore a strip off his shirttail and wrapped the finger.

Then we bent a piece of wire and hooked it into his torn overalls like a safety pin. It kept the tear from getting wider and we hoped it would last until we arrived at his aunt's house in Chicago.

We had not eaten in such a long time that we were very weak and walking was an effort. After we bought our tickets to Chicago, we had less than five dollars left between us. Our money might run out before getting to Frank's aunt. There was a place to buy food in the train station. We stood in line behind white people and waited until they were served, then we bought some cookies. We also bought two bags of salted peanuts, because peanuts encouraged you to drink water and that would keep your stomach full. The cookies were for dessert.

We gobbled down the peanuts, saving a few for the train ride, then looked for the "Colored" drinking fountain. We walked through the station searching for it, while at the same time trying not to appear too conspicuous. "White" fountains seemed to be all over the place, but we didn't see one marked for Black folks. We became a little desperate. After having eaten the peanuts, we had to have the water to drink or we would soon be hungry again. Also the train was scheduled to leave at any moment. Finally, we asked one of the shoeshine boys, a man in his sixties, where the "Colored" fountain was located.

"Broke down two days ago," he replied. "They ain't fixed it yet. Want some water, go back into the bathroom over yonder and drink from the tap, which ain't running too good either."

We stood there, bewildered. White people all about us went to the fountains and drank and then went on. If we rushed back to the bathroom, we would run the risk of missing the train. We decided against the water, hoping maybe we could get some on the train. We went outside where people were already gathered around the train. Black people waited near the engine, where steam hissed and billowed into the air. A secret smile seemed to be on their faces. This was the train that would take us North!

"All aboard!" called the conductor. I felt a smile coming into my eyes. I forgot my empty stomach and my sore finger. Soon, at last, I would be on a train that would take me directly to Chicago! I kept looking back over my shoulder, praying that nothing would stop me this time. The line was moving and the Black folks began boarding the segregated coach behind the engine. Frank's eyes were shining. "Man, we is on our way, but looks like we gonna smell them cinders again!"

What did I care about cinders? Even if they didn't have water on the train, that wouldn't bother me either. I felt like the slaves must have felt years ago when they crossed out of the United States into Canada, like the Spanish Republicans as they later escaped Franco, and like the Jews as they evaded the storm troopers of Hitler. I felt as though I could do without water all the way to Chicago.

Chapter 3

Chicago

The train trip from Covington, Kentucky lasted for ten hours. Along the way I fell sound asleep. When I woke up everyone around me was laughing and talking and even singing. The train had slowed almost to a halt. I got a brief glimpse of buildings climbing toward the sky before we eased into the station. Chicago? How long had I been asleep? I heard Frank laughing and talking up a storm with the other Black folks in the coach. The pure joy shining on his face had transformed it. The haunted look that previously shadowed his eyes had disappeared. He pranced up and down the aisle in his raggedy overalls. Even the tone of his voice seemed to have deepened. For the first time I noticed a moustache was beginning to sprout above his lips. "Naw, naw, naw," he was saying to someone. "I don't want me no Buick. I want a Studebaker. Best car on the road. A Ford and Chevy can't get nowhere close to it!"

"That's 'cause it so slow! Ford and Chevy pass it so fast and leave it covered in so much dust, they can't even see a Studebaker for them to get close."

"Well, y'all got to get jobs first. Otherwise, you'll be lucky to afford to buy a pair of roller skates."

"We're here," Frank shouted at me when he saw I was awake. "Windy city, Chi...ca...go!"

Frank's dark brown face screwed itself up in a deep, serious look. "Great big ball of fire! Blocked the path of the train. Blocked everything in sight. Ain't that right, y'all?"

Voices chorused: "Yes. Yes. Never seen such a ball of fire in all my born days."

"Like the fiery furnace."

"Fire?" I said. I had never imagined the Mason-Dixon line to be fire. A mountain, maybe, or perhaps even a river, but not fire. I looked at them skeptically, "Then how did we get through it?"

Frank paced the aisle expansively as he explained, "Well, the gates opened up. 'Lectrified gates. And once the train shot through, the gates closed behind us again. And don't you know, they had colored men manning them gates. Nothing can get through and up North that they don't want. Ain't that right, y'all?"

The others laughed heartily and lied right along with Frank. "Most 'lectrified gates you ever seen! And them big colored gentlemen in charge was mean. Ain't likely they'd let a single cracker come through them gates, less he done changed his ways. Boy, you shoulda stayed awake, that's all."

"Chi...ca...go!"

"Hallelujah!"

"Get me a job and start living a little."

"Not a little. A whole lot."

"How long did I sleep?" I asked Frank. "You shoulda woke me up." We were filing out of the coach. The people continued to laugh and jostle each other. I couldn't remember being around a group of Black people who seemed so happy.

"Tried to. But you wouldn't wake up for nothing."

I reckoned not. I'd just have to write Papa and tell him I'd missed seeing the Mason-Dixon line, but that it was still out there somewhere and maybe I'd get a chance to see it one day.

Frank walked with his shoulders pulled back and laughed loud good-byes to the other folks when we got inside the station. I caught myself laughing a lot, too. Then we were alone and some of Frank's bravado vanished. As we advanced into the station we saw no one wearing old dirty overalls like us. And certainly no one with a big hole gaping at their knee like Frank. Instead, the swiftly moving people, zipping and zapping through the station like they were all going to a fire, were so citified in their dress, it looked like Easter Sunday. Black folks dashed about their business as swiftly as the white folks.

As we walked, our heads kept turning around and we gazed at the folks. Frank stared at a Black man in a brilliant brown suit as though he could feel himself in it. He shook his head in frustration. We came to a water fountain. The brackish water on the colored coach had tasted like it was a month old. We stared at the fountain. A white man bent and took a quick sip and kept on going. For an instant Frank eyed me nervously. Then he forced himself to stoop and drank from the fountain. Then I drank. We had a few peanuts left over and we threw them into our mouths and kept on drinking. We sipped the water like it was pot liquor. After a time my stomach felt bloated, but I felt good.

We went into the toilet and stood beside white men and used the urinals. The world didn't come to an end. The white men didn't even seem to see us. They did their business and left. We did the same. It seemed like a miracle. It was so different from what I'd experienced all of my life.

We went outside. My finger throbbed occasionally, but my mind was too full for me to worry about it. Also, when I held my hand at a certain angle, the blood pressure seemed to be less and the pain went away.

The roar of the traffic, the steady hum of the city, reached out and claimed us. Cars were everywhere —Model T's, Studebakers, Buicks. There were streetcars clanging through the traffic, horses and buggies plodding around the streetcars; people were coming and going from every direction, crowding the sidewalks and moving in and out of the gigantic buildings.

My eyes drank it all in. My ears listened to this new music of the city. As I stood there, I pinched myself to make sure it was real—could this be me, a country boy, in the middle of such a magic place!

"Watch out," Frank shouted. The brakes of a streetcar screeched in my ears. I jumped out of its path. It brushed by me so close I could see each and every face inside. The blue eyes of a woman turned and raked me over without any particular interest as a car sped by and stopped. Just some fool who'd nearly gotten himself run down. Frank held onto my arm. He was shaking too.

"Better watch out how these crazy folks drive. If you don't hurry and get out of the way, look like they'll run smack over you."

We weren't sure what streetcar to catch to take us to Frank's aunt's house, but we ran and joined a line of people and caught the first one that came. From habit we headed toward the back of the streetcar, but then Frank shot a glance at me and we stopped in our tracks. We saw other Blacks plopping themselves down wherever they wanted. We stood by a white lady. There was an empty seat next to her. I didn't know if she was the same one who'd looked out the window or not. But I knew she was white.

"Well, go ahead and sit," I heard myself tell Frank. "I ain't tired."

"I ain't tired either," Frank replied.

"You must be," I said. "You didn't sleep on the train as long as I did."

"Naw, I ain't tired. I rested real good on the train."

For some reason we were whispering.

"But," I said, "if you didn't sleep, you must be tired." A type of anger entered my voice. "You must be scared," I accused him.

Frank glared back at me. "I ain't scared of shit! I'd sit down in a minute if I wanted to. You scared!"

We stood there glaring at one another. It was confusing. We might drink from the water fountains, go to the toilets, but getting close to a white woman was a different thing. In the South it would have meant death.

So we just stood there, shifting from one foot to the other. Neither one of us sat. The woman couldn't have cared less. She never looked up.

"We could be lost, anyway. Maybe this streetcar don't go past Forty-third." Forty-third was where his aunt lived. Suddenly I was very eager to get there.

Frank squared his shoulders and led the way to the front of the streetcar while saying to me, "We ought to ask the conductor, I reckon." But the conductor seemed irritated when Frank addressed him. He spoke in a rapid Northern-sounding way. Frank kept saying, "Suh?" over and over, not understanding him. A Black passenger finally interceded, and he told us to get off the streetcar and transfer to another car because Forty-third was in the opposite direction from the way in which we were traveling.

We got off and caught the right streetcar, which ran parallel to the railroad tracks. Outside, the neighborhood began to look worse. A strange sickly odor, like burnt flesh just beginning to rot, grew stronger in the air. Small run-down houses bordered the tracks. The people coming in and out of the houses were white. I suspected that if we kept on riding, we would soon come to where Black folks lived. Blacks always seemed to live on the other side of railroad tracks.

But how could Frank's aunt live near the railroad tracks if she was rich? She should be living in the better part of the city. Or were the rich and the poor, if they were Black, forced to live together, even here in Chicago? "Must be going in the wrong direction again," Frank said, gazing out the window uneasily. "Don't look too hot out there."

"Naw," I said, "the numbers' getting bigger. We are going the right way. Maybe the streets gonna git richer-looking up ahead."

"Them letters she wrote home," Frank continued anxiously, "said she was gitting along better than the Queen of Sheba. It looks pretty bad out there."

"Well, that must be where the poor white folks live. It probably gonna git real rich-looking real soon."

"I sure hope so," Frank said. But it didn't. Suddenly, inside, Black folks were everywhere. The composition of the streetcar had been changing gradually. From a majority white, the car was now almost completely Black. And many Blacks swarmed the streets outside, standing before buildings and leaning from windows, thronging the sidewalks. It was as though we'd crossed another Mason-Dixon line.

A sort of electric rhythm had come into the air. People were bursting at the seams with vitality. Music blared into the streets from the churches or the pool-halls. Somewhere Bessie Smith was singing "Crazy Blues." From another direction I heard her voice moaning "The Muscle Shoals Blues." The sound of Louis Armstrong's trumpet could be heard. Tambourines were being beaten vigorously inside one of the churches. A few people snapped their fingers as they bounced down the street, others strutted and wore their hats tilted at rakish angles, while ladies strutted by in tight dresses.

For a moment Frank and I forgot about his aunt. We stared out the streetcar window, gripped by this great Black world within the world of Chicago. Beyond these people, we sensed the presence of thousands of other Blacks, and, it is said there were even more Blacks in Harlem, New York.

"Look at that fellow," Frank shouted. "See, gittin' into that Studebaker? See! See that gal he's with? Man, folks is living up here!"

I saw the Studebaker. I saw the man and the girl getting into the new shiny car, a man in a suit so pea-green, it looked yellowish. But I also saw that most of the people didn't look as prosperous as those two, and the buildings were more run-down than those in the white section that we had just come through.

The excitement of the new city claimed us and we made the mistake of getting off at Fortieth Street instead of Forty-third. Frank stared at the poor looking surroundings and was silent as we walked the three blocks to Forty-third.

Once at Forty-third Street, we had little trouble finding his aunt's place, which was located above a delicatessen. The smell of pickles, mixed with the rancid odor that seemed to have been following us ever since we arrived in Chicago, clung to the entrance. We climbed the rickety stairs enveloped in a strong scent of urine. We reached his aunt's apartment door. From inside we heard the sound of children being scolded.

Frank let out a deep breath. "Could still be the wrong place. Maybe I ought to have written and told her I was coming and then she coulda sent us better directions. . . ." He stopped. He knew it was the right place. He knocked heavily.

"Who is it?" a woman's voice yelled. "I ain't buying a damn thing, so don't bother me when . . ." She snatched the door open. Her face expressed shock at the sight of Frank. Her eyes blinked in embarrassment. "Frank, boy, what you doing in the big city!"

She was a large woman and her brown skin bulged out of her calico dress. Her accent still sounded more like down home than up here in the city. She threw her arms around Frank and hugged him tightly. She gave me a hug too. But I noticed the embarrassment returning as she invited us into the overcrowded two-room apartment.

Three or four children were in the room. It wasn't at all like the rich place she'd written home about.

Frank concealed his disappointment by laughing a lot and bringing his aunt up to date on what was happening down in Quitman. The aunt shook her head sadly. "Them crackers down there just ain't gone' never change." She had sent one of the older children out to buy some fresh greens. In the small kitchen she was now heating up some chitterlings and she was baking a sweet potato pie. "And up here, they ain't much better either," she added.

"But this is Chicago," Frank protested. He kept glancing about the small, crowded room as if he still thought he might be in the wrong place. "Crazy peckerwoods don't lynch you or nothing up here. And I saw folks out there getting into... getting into new Studebakers... And ...and... your letters... well, I thought you had to be doing real good, too, up here."

The aunt wiped her hands on a dishrag and reeled around, looking angrily at Frank.

"I ain't doing so bad. I'm raising my children. They ain't got to fear nobody. In them letters I wrote . . . in them letters . . . well, I never said I was doing as good as the Wrigleys. But I'm getting by. I'm raising my children."

Frank couldn't find his tongue. Even as we got our feet under the table and started dipping into the greens and chitterlings, he said nothing. I was silent, too, eating my meal slowly.

When Frank finished, he suddenly said, with determination, "Well, first thing tomorrow morning I'm going out there and get myself a job. In no time at all I'm gone' have myself set up. Get me two or three suits and a car and . . ."

His aunt looked at him and spoke softly, "Better learn to crawl before you start all that walking and running. You just don't go out the door and pick up a good job off the street."

"Maybe at Wrigleys'," I said. "Is Wrigleys' hiring anybody? We Black folks chew lots of gum."

"If you ain't colored, they hiring. Even the porters to mop the floors over there is white. Must be them Wrigleys just can't stand the sight of colored folks."

"Then where we gone' get jobs?" Frank wanted to know. "Where's all this rich stuff in Chicago everybody been talking about?"

"Stockyard, maybe. You catch that smell in the air? Well, that's where it comes from. I hear it's hard working over there, but they always seem to need new hands."

Frank went back into his gloomy silence. I thanked his aunt for the meal and told her I should go out and look for a room to rent for myself.

"Nonsense," she said. "Don't talk no nonsense. You homefolks. You and Frank stay right here till you get on your feet. That is, if you don't mind sleeping on pallets and putting up with the noise these doggone children make. But usually I get them to sleep early, so they ought not bother y'all too much."

I was so grateful, I could have hugged her. Frankly, at sixteen I was still a bit scared of going out there into the big city all alone. I would find a job first and then rent a room nearby if I could. Frank might be disappointed in his aunt, but I liked her. With my own folks so far away, it would be comforting to have someone like her nearby.

Frank finished his third slice of pie. "Sure was good," he admitted grudgingly. He looked at his aunt as though he might one day forgive her for pretending to be richer than she really was.

Frank wanted us to find clean jobs as stockboys, porters, or maybe we'd even be lucky and somebody would hire us as bellhops or waiters. We wasted more than a week looking for good jobs like that, until I got panicky and told him I was ready to go to the stockyard, smell or no smell. I would have liked to have been hired as a bellhop or waiter, but those jobs were at the very top of the list for Black people. Once you got such a position, you were considered "somebody." But we had no experience and knew no one to help us get such jobs. In any case, most of them were already covered by the older men.

Reluctantly, Frank came with me to the stockyard. The closer we got, the worse the smell became. It was no longer a smell in the air. It was the air! It seeped into our clothes and clung to our skin. I imagined long lines of people slamming huge sledgehammers against the skulls of cattle to kill them, then boiling the bodies. The burning of the hair of the flesh caused the sickening odor. My father told stories of Black men being roasted alive in the South. As we came into the stockyard, I knew the smell of those men must have been much like this. I wanted to vomit even before I stepped inside the gates.

We went into the office. White ladies sat behind typewriters. A white man, bustling all over the place, seemed to be the supervisor.

One lady shoved some forms toward us and told us to fill them out. I labored over my bad writing. I glanced at the intense concentration on Frank's face as he attempted to understand the forms. We both wrote like chickens scratching. When the young lady who took back the forms had trouble understanding what we wrote, my ears burned with shame. The young lady easily completed filling in the forms for us. I looked at her beautiful handwriting and longed for the day I would be able to write like that.

The busy white man zipped over to the counter, glanced at the forms and hired us on the spot. His eyes were so busy, they were already running back to something else he thought he should be doing. He hurled instructions at us. "Go out that door and through the yard. Ask for Thomas or Mr. Crodowsky."

"Suh?"

"Mr. Crodowsky."

I had never heard such a long and funny name, and I surely had never been called upon to pronounce anything like it before. I tried to keep the name firmly in my mind, hoping I would know how to say who it was I was looking for.

Without really looking at us, the man said: "Tell them to put you in the freezer. You think you can handle the freezer?"

We didn't know what he was talking about, but we both said: "Yessuh."

We went out. Inside the office the odor had been faint, but as we opened the door to leave it rushed at us again. I felt like I was sucking burnt hairs through my nostrils. We were in a large concrete courtyard surrounded by shiny new-looking buildings. Black smoke belched from chimneys. Small tractors hummed as they pulled carts from one building to another. A number of Black men were bent low over pushcarts. One came by, wheeling his load of meat and bones, and a thick trail of blood dripped from the cart. Swarms of green flies pursued the cargo.

A blazing sun pierced the heavy smoke, laden with odors wafting from the shiny buildings. I wondered what was inside those buildings. Perhaps they had electric hammers rather than sledgehammers to kill the cattle. I imagined I could see the animals cringing in terror. I hoped Frank and I wouldn't be assigned where we'd have to watch the killing.

Trying to avoid having to ask one of the white workers for directions, we stopped an aging Black man who was pushing a blood splattered broom in the wake of the carts. He pointed toward a stocky broad-shouldered white man and we crossed the yard toward him.

Mr. Cradowsky didn't look around at us immediately. He was busy giving orders to two other Black workers, or trying to. His accent was so strange and thick, I had trouble understanding what he was saying. In frustration, Mr. Crodowsky pointed toward a building from which I thought I heard cattle bawling. The two men walked away muttering. Mr. Crodowsky turned to us and his cheeks

were flushed bright red. Though his eyes were blue and his hair a sort of rough dirty blond, his lips were as full as most Black people's. He took our assignment order and stared at it. He looked at it so long, I wondered if he could read. He said something like, "Freeza?
    "Suh?"
    He used his hands, pointing at us, desperate to be understood. "You. You. Freeza?"
    I supposed he meant "freezer," whatever that was, whatever the man in the office had meant. So I said, "Yassuh."
    "Sure?" He gazed at us doubtfully. I wondered what was the matter. Was he trying to maneuver us out of our jobs? Were the whites here in Chicago, despite funny names with different accents, the same as most of the crackers I'd known in the South?
    "Yassuh, I'm sure." I was ready to go back to the office and fight for my job. He frowned uncertainly, then turned and led us into one of the buildings. We got on an elevator. I held myself tense, expecting it to zoom upwards, but it plunged downwards. The motion caught us so off guard that Frank clutched his stomach and gasped. I held onto the wall. I knew about elevators that went up, but I had never heard of one that went down into the ground. After a long while, it came to a halt and we stepped out into a hazy, vaporish world. It had to be many degrees below freezing. The bitter cold sliced at me and nearly cut off my breath. The temperature above was at least ninety degrees. Now it felt as though we had been deposited at the North Pole. Crystals of pure ice floated in the air.
    Men moved before us like ghosts. Dressed in bulky sweaters, coats, and leather aprons, with only their eyes exposed, and using meat hooks, they slammed icy slabs of cattle around the room. One cow, its eyes still gaping in terror, green flies still embedded in its frozen flesh, broke loose from a hook and skidded toward us. Frank and I almost jumped back into the elevator.

I heard my teeth chattering. I could see my breath.

Dressed in only our shirts, overalls, and light under-clothes, Frank and I were certainly not dressed for a place like this.

Mr. Crodowsky took two hooks down from a rack and was about to give them to us when he hesitated and looked at our clothes and our faces. Frank drew close to me for warmth. He shook so violently that we were trembling as one.

Mr. Crodowsky placed the hooks back where he found them. Then he said to us, "Come."   He led us back onto the elevator. He stared at us. He made a very great effort to make himself understood. "Go back office. Say, too cold. Too cold. Maybe get other works."

I found my voice,"Yassuh." I wanted to thank him, but didn't know quite what to say, or if he would understand my Mississippi accent.

"Good!" He seemed tremendously relieved that he had made this decision. We came up into the blistering heat. The putrid smell that had been frozen below attacked us again. A tall, thin Black man, limping heavily and favoring his left side, came up to us. He had a large balding head and angry brown eyes. "You damn Polack!" he said to Mr. Crodowsky. "What'er you doing with these two boys?" Then he glared at us. "I'm Thomas. Why didn't you boys ask to see me?"

Mr. Crodowsky tried to speak. His whole face had reddened. I was stunned. I had never heard a Black man speak so contemptuously to a white man before. Thomas shook his finger in Mr. Crodowsky's face. "Keep out of my jurisdiction! I ain't gone' tell you no more to stop fucking with my jurisdiction!"

The anger that Mr. Crodowsky did not know how to express caused his strong body to tremble. For some reason, I felt sorry for him. He said something in a language I didn't understand.

"Speak American, sonofabitch!" Thomas shouted. "If these had been white boys, would you have took them down there in that cold hell? Look how they is dressed. I don't care what the office say. You shouldn't have took them down there into that icebox."

"The office boss. Not you!" Mr. Crodowsky shouted back. In fairness, I wanted to tell Thomas that it wasn't Mr. Crodowsky's fault. He didn't think we were supposed to work in the freezer either.

"C'mon with me, boys," Thomas commanded. "Leave the little Pope bossman to hisself." We followed Thomas. I stole a look back at Mr. Crodowsky. A few other workers had witnessed the· scene. He was so embarrassed, he looked like he wanted to find a hole in the ground to crawl into. I don't know why he reminded me of Mr. Joe in Quitman, and of the white hobo on the train. It was the first time in my life it had occurred to me that there might be white people in the world as weak and powerless as I was.

"Stupid Polack!" Thomas's anger still boiled in his tone. A vein beat violently in his neck. Though he limped, we had to almost trot to keep up with him. "Just got off the boat and gone' tell me who's boss! Come here from Polack country where he was too ignorant for them other Polacks to even train him to pick potatoes and cabbage.

Now he means to boss me! I been on this job nineteen years. Even that boy in there in the office couldn't find his ass from a hole in the ground if I wasn't out here for him to call on and git help. And he went to Harvard! Boys, I'm tellin you," he ranted on, "don't trust no crackers, North or South, them that's born here or them that's shipped in. Nineteen years I been here and they still act like they don't know my last name." He stopped in front of one of the shiny buildings. His chest heaved like he was trying to put out a furnace burning inside himself. Outrage reddened his brown eyes, but he got his breath, softened his voice and asked, "Where you boys from?"

"Mississippi," Frank answered first. He stared at Thomas in fascination, almost fear.

"An evil state. Evil! Texas, myself. Twenty-three years ago come here from Texas. On the outskirts of town they had a colored man hanged from a church steeple. In the very place they were going to go and pray to their white god that Sunday they had strung a colored man up." His eyes grew even redder as he reminisced, "I caught me a freight train and didn't stop till I got to Chicago. You boys heard of the Movement?"

"Suh?"

"The U.N.I.A.?"

Frank said brightly, "Like the Elks or Masons? I always been thinking I'd like to join up with something like that."

For a second Thomas's face was still, but then it boiled again and a vein popped out on his dark brown forehead. "Black ignorance! There is no excuse for Black ignorance! We got chapters of the Universal Negro Improvement Association throughout the country. Your heads been so buried in cotton sacks, you ain't heard nothing. Every intelligent colored man in the country knows of our movement and our leader. Ain't you ever heard of Marcus Garvey?"

I wasn't sure. I thought maybe Professor Blakeney had mentioned him. Then I remembered the letter from my uncle to my father about the Marcus Garvey Movement. He had written that he was waiting for a boat to take him to Africa. But Thomas was so excited, I decided not to say a word. "Boys, this is a movement to get us back to Africa, away from these evil white folks. Get us to a continent where we was once kings and queens! Builders of empires! Now, I'm gone' get y'all onto a good job making sausage and frankfurters. But as soon as you settled in, I'm gone' stop by one evening and pick you up and take you to one of our meetings. Boys, you'll git that ignorance out of your head. Learn that till we git back to Mother Africa, there ain't gone' be no freedom for us. Now come with me."

We followed him inside where huge paddles whirled inside giant vats. Men used smaller paddles to keep the mass of grinding meat and bones moving. Some vats had spilled over and the floor was slippery with blood and half-ground meat. Green flies had penetrated the building and the men brushed them away from their faces as they stirred the vats.

"This Wop here will look after you," Thomas said. He brought us to a vat watched over by a short, fat white man with jet-black hair. "Victorio, you take care of these two boys. And look after them right. Or I'll come back in here and kick your Wop ass."

Victorio wore a big grin. It was possible he didn't understand a word Thomas said. He mopped his face with a handkerchief. He leaned over the vat and listened to Thomas. The dirty handkerchief fell in and went sailing with the meat around the giant paddle, then down into the meat. When Victorio looked for his handkerchief, he couldn't find it. He kept grinning.

I brushed a fly from my face. "Your job is to help keep the vats full," Thomas instructed us. Then he limped purposefully across the greasy, bloody floor, as though he had some special and very important place to go.

Chapter 4

Bessie

An unshakable loneliness ate into me around the time of my fourth Christmas in Chicago. I was about twenty-one years old and I longed to see my family. I needed more friends, or maybe a wife, to help ward off the cold, granite-hard city. There were four and five days in a row when I had no one to talk with, except for those at work. I remembered those nights back home when I sat with my family before the fireplace and roasted peanuts and sweet potatoes. I could have screamed for some human being to step inside my four bare walls and break this terrible Northern silence.

I grabbed my coat and buttoned up against the freezing weather, then rushed across the city looking for Frank. I found him in a dingy speakeasy sipping from a drink and eyeing the ladies.

"I'm going back home," I said.

"Man, you crazy."

"Maybe no one will bother us down there any more, if we mind our own business."

"Well, don't look at me. I sure ain't going with you. I ain't even going back for a visit. I'm getting me a new Studebaker next month. Imagine what them crackers gone' act like if I come down there driving a brand new car! Have you forgotten what happened to those Black soldiers coming home from overseas after World War I? Some were almost lynched for breaking the law set by the local authorities when they were wearing their uniforms after more than three days. Just the other week I heard where they lynched another colored man down in Tupelo, Mississippi."

I sat down. Frank offered me a drink and I took it. I stared at the raw alcohol colored by Coca-Cola before draining the glass. I listened to the ladies laughing and didn't say anything for a moment. Then I said, "Maybe I can get a gun."

"What?" Frank said.

"A gun. Take a gun in case I run into some kind of trouble."

"You serious? You must be crazy. What yo' little one gun gone' to do against all their guns? Minute you forgot to say, 'yassuh' or 'nawsuh,' they'll be on top of you like white on rice. You won't even get a chance to pull out your gun."

"But I got to go, Frank. Gun or no gun. A man ought to have the right to go see his own family. If you won't help me find a gun, I'll ask somebody else. I done made up my mind."

Frank was silent. He twirled the glass in his hand. His two large gaudy rings that passed themselves off as diamonds glittered dully. He frowned and shook his head.

"I know how you feel. Sometimes I feel real bad, too, when I think of my family. But I can't go back." He lifted his glass and finished it. "I think you crazy. But if I can't talk you out of going back, I guess I can speak to one of my buddies about finding you a gun."

"When?"

"When you want it?"

"Soon as you can get it."

He said it shouldn't take too long, a day or two, maybe. We had another drink. Then I buttoned up against the cold and went out into the white snowy city.

Instead of a gun, Frank brought a girl. I heard the horn blowing and rushed to the window. The new car was a lively green with whitewall tires. Frank's suit and hat and overcoat looked as though they'd been bought to match the car. I stared in amazement. Frank had got the new car he wanted so much.

He grandly helped the girl out of the car. I was curious, but I hoped she was not one of those barflies I saw him talk with before. He knew my landlady wouldn't be happy with that. She was barely tolerant if I brought a "respectable" girl by for a visit. And then I'd better get the girl out of my room before ten o'clock at night.

Well, instead of a gun, he had brought me a girl. As I opened the door, I received a jolt. I gazed at a tall, dark, brown-skinned girl who really didn't look at all like a tramp. There was a ladylike quality about her. Except for the thin winter coat that the wind whipped ruthlessly about her, she was dressed in the fashion of the young ladies who attended the Methodist Church. I wondered where Frank had found such a girl.

They came in, the young lady's teeth chattering. She shivered from the cold. Frank was expansive. He stripped off his white gloves and rubbed the cold from his cheeks and ears.

"The hawk is out!"

"And biting everything in sight!" the girl added.

I stared at the girl. Why did she look so familiar? I rushed them into my room. I was happy that my landlady had put some flowers in the vase that morning.

"He doesn't remember me," the young lady laughed. "You better tell him."

She was almost as tall as I was and nicely built.

"I ought not tell him nothing," Frank said, teasingly. "In fact, we can go right now, 'cause I wouldn't have brought you out here at all to visit this dummy if you hadn't kept insisting."

She smiled at me. There was a certain shyness in her smile, but it lit up her big eyes and round brown face. Suddenly I knew who she was, but I simply couldn't believe it.

"Bessie?" I said, but further words failed me. She used to be the little girl who played jacks and Little Sally Walker with my sisters and jumped rope in front of our house, and who heard my mother and father tell that embarrassing tale about the day my Uncle William cut out a cow's tongue and ate it. I became self-conscious in her presence, just like I had when we were children.

"Yes," she said. I hope you don't mind the way I pestered Frank into bringing me to see you. I promised your folks in Quitman I'd look you up."

I murmured something incoherent and rushed to help her out of her coat. I felt her young, adult body still trembling from the cold. Bessie sat and crossed her legs and I sat down near her, trying to think of something intelligent to say. I had completely forgotten about the gun Frank was to bring.

"I arrived three days ago," Bessie said, "in the middle of that snowstorm. I'm staying with my cousin. I had Frank's aunt's address and she told me how to find Frank and today he finally brought me to see you. So, here I am."

It was pleasant listening to her voice, and I waited for her to go on. But suddenly she seemed shy too. I still didn't know what to say for a moment and then questions about my family began to tumble out of my mouth. How was Mama? Papa? Grandmama? My sisters? Bessie said they were all okay, except my father had fallen and broken a rib while repairing the house. But he was all right now. He sent his love and thanks for the postcards I mailed him regularly.

"And Elijah?" I asked. "He left home with Frank and me, but his dad pulled him off the train at Stonewall." "Oh," she said, "he is gone again. I was sure expecting to see him here in Chicago."

I looked at Frank and Frank looked at me. Then he dropped his eyes. Maybe they had arrested Elijah or lynched him . . . but for what? We all knew the crackers didn't need a good reason.

I asked Bessie about young Archie Brown. She explained that he had been gone five years and no one heard from him until a man from the Delta passed through Quitman and stopped at the barbershop managed by Archie's brother. While introducing himself, the man said he knew a Brown from Quitman working on the Delta cotton plantation. The story was that Archie was arrested while riding a freight train. He was bailed out of jail by a plantation owner, and Archie worked on the plantation ever since. The man explained how this method of bailouts was another way of enslaving our people.

"I was planning to visit home," I suddenly blurted.

Bessie looked at me in alarm. "It isn't any better down there, and I don't believe it will ever get any better. I think your folks will understand."

Bessie couldn't find a job and that distressed her. She thought that with her high school diploma she would soon get a very good job, like the white girls in the office at the stockyard. But no luck, she could not even get a sales job. In the Black neighborhoods the stores like Woolworth's didn't have a single Black face behind their counters. Downhearted, Bessie finally took a "temporary" job as a nursemaid to a little white boy in one of the better sections of the city. She knew she would have to wear a ridiculous white nanny's uniform, but hopefully this would be for only a short time. Soon she would find herself a decent job and be on her way to college.

Bessie began to bug me about my work at the stockyard. She was certain I could find a "cleaner," better job if I put more effort into it. Then I would not have to act so ashamed when people asked me what I did.

I had been attempting to get a waiter's job with the Pennsylvania Railroad, and now I redoubled that effort. I was soon hired as a busboy, a waiter being something you worked up to. I told Bessie about my good luck. She did her best to appear impressed. Busboy for a large railroad company was certainly an improvement over working at the filthy, smelly stockyard. But I could see that she was a bit unhappy that I didn't get the waiter's job right off.

I drew close to Bessie, courted Bessie, and pursued Bessie as though my life depended on it.

One happy morning I was promoted to waiter. A waiter at last! An old and ailing Black man had died and I was given his job. Bessie was elated over the promotion. I took the opportunity to get over my nervousness and asked her to marry me. She knew I had been leading up to this and wasn't too surprised. She didn't say yes or no, but just pondered over it a few days and then came to me and threw her arms around me and said "Yes!" That night we celebrated. Bessie said she hoped I understood how badly she wanted to attend a college one day. I said I understood. Well, I thought I did.

Every dining car carried approximately seven waiters, four cooks and a steward. The steward was the boss and enforced the company rules. He was always white. Working conditions for me as a busboy had been terrible, but they weren't much better as a waiter. Though we handled the food, we were not permitted to eat some of the better dishes we served to the mostly white diners. After work we slept practically on top of each other in the dining car. By stacking up the dining tables jailhouse fashion, they became our beds for the night. An unwritten law said we shouldn't wander about the train but must remain in the dining coach. At the end of a trip we could be laid off or have our pay docked if there had been the least infraction of any company rule. A trip under a mean steward could become outright hell.

No one talked of a union, not even in a hushed voice. The Black workers grumbled, but didn't really dare question the fact that a white man was always put over us as boss. For wasn't that the natural order of things? From President Hoover all the way back to the plantation owners during slavery time, hadn't white men wielded the authority? Even some Blacks might have thought it strange and unnatural if the Pennsylvania Railroad had hired a Black as a boss.

There was an incident on one trip from Chicago to Detroit. The steward was the kind of man everyone feared. Over the years he had been the cause of many men losing their jobs because of some slight infraction of the rules. One day I was caught eating a bran muffin. The steward challenged me about this matter. I decided that someone had to make a stand sometime. I grabbed the collar of his white shirt and pushed him out of the kitchen into the dining car. By this time, every waiter was trying nervously to pull me off him.

After the spat I continued with my usual duties on the way back to Chicago. I was sure this would be my last trip with the Pennsylvania Railroad, so I took all my belongings from the diner. The next day I was on my way to collect my pay. Although I figured I was fired, I still took my working uniform of pants, white shirt and black bow tie.

As I stood on the steps of the dining car commissary, the steward passed by along with waiters preparing themselves for their next trip out of town. I did not dare to sign my name on the reporting roster. Looking at my watch, I knew the train would soon be backing into the station. About this time I saw the dispatcher peep his head from the door and yell," Yates, aren't you going to sign up?" I was really surprised. The steward must not have reported our feud. I quickly jotted my name and rushed across the tracks to the dining car. I never heard a word about the tussle between myself and the steward. From that day on the steward treated me with respect. The waiters and cooks came up to me in a hushed manner, still not believing that I was with them. They showed much more respect when I talked with them about joining the union. Bessie quit the nursemaid job that she held in contempt. She was certain she could find a very good job once she could write on her application that she was attending college. She was expecting a baby now and planned to go back to school after the birth. I think she would rather have waited a little longer before starting a family. But now that the baby was on the way, she was as excited as I was. We would simply work a bit harder and one day soon we would be able to buy a little house in a suburb of Chicago and a good car. Not one as flashy as Frank's, but something we would certainly be proud to own. The future looked bright and we were confident. Every time I returned home, an unending feeling of love and affection seemed to deepen between Bessie and me. Our daughter, Louise, was born on October 15, 1928. I was happier than I had ever been in my life. But that was soon to change.

On a bright sunny morning in 1929 our train from Madison, Wisconsin, pulled into a station a few miles from Chicago. As usual, complimentary copies of Chicago newspapers were picked up for the passengers. The dining car was filled with people sipping their second cups of coffee. We waiters bowed as we handed each passenger a paper, hoping it would enhance the tip. Suddenly, as they glanced at the headlines, cups fell and crashed onto the tables. Men shot up from their seats. Others ran from the diner to the train conductor demanding a telephone. I looked at the headline which read, *"Stock Market Crash."* It made no sense to me. One young waiter shook his head and remarked "Crazy white folks acting like the world done come to an end."

The panic was contagious. I noticed that our steward collapsed in the kitchen and the cook had to catch him from falling on the hot stove. I looked around and saw one of the waiters weeping. He often talked with the steward about the stock market and always listened eagerly for advice. I wondered why he was crying; it was the white folks that had lost their money, not us. But later I learned that he had good enough reason to be upset. His savings over the last forty years were now gone.

Not until I reached Chicago did I know the real effect of the crisis. Radios and newspapers reported panic on Wall Street. Already several stockbrokers had jumped from tall buildings on New York's Wall Street. A large number of people were pointing pistols at their heads.

My bank closed like all the others across the country. But losing my little one hundred dollars wasn't going to make me jump from a train, bridge or building. The crash was a great puzzle to me. It was something white people allowed to get out of hand temporarily; since Black people had no power or authority to rectify the situation, we would simply have to wait until the whites in control straightened out the whole mess.

They almost didn't pull the country out of it. The stock market failure signalled the beginning of the worst depression the United States had ever known. Bessie believed even more passionately than I that the good times were coming back. In a sense she refused to accept the fact that they had vanished. The more my tips dwindled, the more she seemed compelled to spend. She wouldn't quit talking about the house we were going to buy and the new car we would be riding in soon. Her eyes assumed some of the bright, glazed look of some of my customers. Sometimes I came home and didn't have the heart to tell her that my tips that day were worse than on the trip before. One evening I blew up. "Is that a new dress?"

"It was a bargain."

"I don't care what kind of bargain it was. We ain't got the money to pay for it no more. From now on you better buy some cheaper material and make your own dresses." Bessie got angry out of proportion to what I thought I'd said.

"I make the baby's clothes. I sew. I scrimp. I'm pinching pennies while you' away not thinking about us! I buy one dress in six months and you yell at me. What do you want me to wear, a cotton sack?"

I didn't realize that I had yelled, but I knew I was angry about the dress. On my last three-day trip, the total of my tips was under four dollars. "Say what you want," I said. "I ain't paying for no more dresses."

Bessie walked away from me and into the tiny kitchen. The baby was asleep on the sofa which expanded into a bed at night. Her crib was in the corner where she slept when Bessie and I used the bed.

I followed Bessie into the kitchen, trying to control my anger. It wasn't her fault that money was becoming so tight. Still, I knew I had to explain to her that we had to go on a budget like we had never known before. It became more apparent that the Depression was not going to end tomorrow, nor any time soon. She kept her back to me and suddenly I saw that she was crying. She held onto the old sink where the water sometimes ran and sometimes didn't, and her shoulders shook violently. She was saying something, but the tears so muffled her voice, I could not understand. I stood there feeling ashamed of myself for having shouted at her. She turned her tear-streaked face toward me, wiping her eyes. "I don't care about the dress. I don't care at all about the dress." She spoke as if she'd been wrestling for several days with whatever she was trying to say. "But I was worried about our getting the house, thinking maybe we'd never get it."

"We'll get it!" I assured her. "I was thinking maybe we weren't going to ever get anything anymore. I didn't even want the dress that much."

"It's all right."

"No. It's not! "I'll take it back. Because . . ."

"You don't have to."

"Because it's not the dress. It's not the car either. But I hope nothing on this earth stops us from getting ourselves a house."

"We'll get it. Times gone' git better!" I insisted.

"I sure hope they do."

"They will." I put my arms around her. I kissed the tears on her face. I looked into her eyes and didn't know why there was so much fear in them. She hugged me tightly for a moment, hesitated, then said, "I sure hope they do. We just got to have that house now. I'm pregnant again."

I felt myself stiffen against her. "What did you say? Another baby?" I couldn't believe the news, on top of everything else. But I didn't want to hurt Bessie any more. I kissed her and said nothing.

The railroad made another severe cutback. I and a number of other waiters were laid off. We joined the thousands, and soon millions, of unemployed across the country. I returned to the stockyard hoping for my old job, but men were being trimmed from the payroll there too. Many of them stood outside the gates peering past the company guards, desperate to get rehired. I saw a bewildered Crodowsky in that crowd, using his broad shoulders as buffers to stay at the head of the line. I also saw a number of Black men who used to sweep the yards and pushed the bloody meat carts. It was senseless to join the line. I went looking for porter jobs, dishwashing jobs, any kind of a job, but suddenly everything had dried up. "Closed" and "Gone Out Of Business" signs hung in the windows of stores and restaurants that had been doing good business only a few months before. Banks locked their doors too. It was shocking, unbelievable, that institutions as sacred as banks could become vacated and lifeless. Bessie and I lost our hundred dollars, every cent we had. We believed in banks so much that we hadn't rushed to withdraw our money.

For several months I roamed the Chicago streets looking for work, still full of crazy hope. I simply couldn't believe there was never going to be a job again. But the growing line of men that queued up for the most demeaning work began to dampen my optimism. One morning I spotted two Black schoolteachers and a lawyer competing with each other for a window washing job that paid ten cents a window. That same afternoon I saw the assistant Methodist minister elbowing his way through a line, competing to unload garbage trucks at fifteen cents a ton. Such were the conditions that existed when my son, Richard, was born on November 19, 1930.

Before he was born, Bessie had returned to her old nursemaid's job. This time she was also required to scrub floors, cook and do the washing. I felt like a worm each time I thought of her in the white lady's kitchen, her fingers dipped into the dirty clothing of strangers and wearing that uniform she hated so much. But without the meager money and leftover food she brought home, we would not have eaten nor have been able to pay the rent. Around the house she grew increasingly moody and silent. I made every effort to keep our own home going and comfortable and our daughter out of her way when she came in irascible and exhausted. Sometimes I thought she looked at me as though it was my fault that I couldn't find work. Often, as if from nowhere, arguments sprang up between us. At other times, we climbed into bed so dispirited we didn't even say good night but turned our backs to each other.

I lost my temper and was ready to fight a man over a dishwashing job. He kept inching up in the line of men around me and shouldering his way to the door of the restaurant. When we looked at him he seemed to be standing still, but the instant we glanced away he would sneak a couple more steps forward again. When the restaurant owner opened the door to pick one of us as dishwasher, he was the first to raise his hand and draw immediate attention to himself. "Me! Over here, suh! I got experience!" We grumbled in the line. Who in the hell did he think he was, jumping ahead of everybody? I vaguely remember having seen him before in other lines and at a couple of the soup kitchens. He was a bit taller, heavier and darker than I was. On those occasions he had seemed to be a dignified and intelligent young man, very quiet with penetrating black eyes. In contrast to the listless unemployed men around him, he was always thumbing through a book. But now his jaws had gone slack and there was an almost idiotic Uncle Tom grin on his face. His shoulders slouched as he stood before the white restaurant owner in total servility. Instantly the owner responded with stinging condescension. "You say you got experience, boy? That means you know how to break up more of my dishes than these other colored boys out here?"

"Nawsuh! I washes good. And I don't break no dishes. I got references, suh!"

"References he probably wrote himself," a man near me muttered bitterly, and added "'Well, I just can't bow and grovel to get me a job, no matter what!"

In Washington Park, near the University of Chicago, there was what they called the Bug Club, a soap-box forum for radicals to discuss their views. When I was not looking for a job, I spent hours just listening to the speakers, sometimes Wobblies, Socialists or others saying things with no real meaning. One day at the Bug Club, I walked to the other side of the park, along Fifty-first Street. A crowd had gathered there around a man speaking from a park bench. I stopped to listen, though I could hardly stand on my feet from hunger. A preacher was telling the crowd about the planned march to Springfield, the capital of the State of Illinois. He went on to tell about the many different organizations involved in this demonstration for jobs, home relief for those who had lost their jobs, and social security, something that didn't exist in those days.

When the preacher finished, a young man in his late teens mounted the bench. His name was Claude Lightfoot and he was a young Communist. I was impressed more by his youth and speaking ability than by what he was saying—something about Karl Marx, a new name to me. When he began to speak about the problems of the young unemployed, with a park bench for a bed, I began to get interested.

In the crowd was a man named Nat Dickson, handing out leaflets about the coming march to Springfield. I wanted to know more about the march. Nat invited me to his house, a basement flat on West Forty-seventh Street. Nat invited some of his white friends from the Northwest side, along with several Black friends, including James Roberson, Claude Lightfoot and Dick Wright. At the house, they explained the story of Oliver Law. Oliver was in jail after having been arrested at a demonstration protesting the unemployment crisis. Nat went on to explain that Oliver had been born on a Texas ranch and that he had joined the United States Army at a young age. After serving eight years in the army he came out as a buck-private. Then James Roberts cut in on the conversation. "They did a good job on him in the segregated army." He went on to tell about young Oscar Hunter, who had just arrived in town from Hampton College, West Virginia. "Oh, boy," he said, "they sure made a 'radical' out of him, too."

Within a few years Oliver Law was to become the first Black commander of an almost all-white unit in faraway Spain. I would be there, too, along with Nat Dickson, James Roberson and Oscar Hunter, but I am running ahead of my story.

I arrived early for the march on Springfield that September morning. More than three hundred cars and trucks, and even some carriages drawn by horses, converged on the South Side of Chicago. People from various churches, unions, political parties and universities were assembling at other locations throughout the city. We all came together somewhere around the outskirts of Chicago and journeyed to Springfield. The Illinois miners, five thousand strong, planned to join us on the north side of the state capitol. Then we would enter the city and proceed to the site of the state legislature, chanting and singing our desire for jobs. We started singing labor songs, but when they struck up "When the Saints Go Marching In," I caught the fever and found myself singing with a passion I hadn't felt for years. People in other trucks and cars picked up that song and it soared in volume. I shivered with pleasure. Suddenly I felt as one with these people, Black and white. I was a part of their hopes, their dreams, and they were a part of mine. And we were a part of an even larger world of marching poor people. By now I understood that the Depression was world-wide and that the unemployed and the poor were demonstrating and agitating for jobs and food all over the globe. We were millions. We couldn't lose. My throat swelled with pride. I sang loud enough for all of Chicago to hear.

As we drove through the small towns, we showered the local people with our leaflets and songs. Some closed their stores, others left their jobs or unemployment lines to join us. Late that night we pulled into farmhouses where arrangements had been made for us to sleep. The women and the children were quartered in the houses, and rows of men wrapped up in blankets and sleeping bags slept in the fields or in the barns. Nat and Jim Roberson joked with Poindexter, telling him he snored like somebody calling hogs. Shortly the fresh country air lulled all of us into such a deep sleep that we didn't know who snored the loudest.

We awoke early in the morning and built a huge fire in the pasture and breakfasted on coffee and rolls. The spirit of the people was higher than ever. As the convoy moved out, we again broke into songs.

We were still a good distance from Springfield when we received the news that the coal miners had been blocked by the National Guard from joining us. Our caravan stopped for a moment, but then the leaders decided to move on. We sang louder to cover our uneasiness. Husbands drew closer to their wives and children. Able-bodied men also readied themselves to protect the women, children and older folks. We were instructed not to fight back if attacked, but to use our bodies to shield those who couldn't help themselves.

We could almost make out the skyline of Springfield when the highway passed through an area with a thick grove of trees on one side and fields on the other. Here the convoy was once again halted. Fresh trees had been cut and placed across the highway as a roadblock. We sat there nervously, not knowing what to do. Then we climbed down and began to remove the roadblock, singing all the while.

We didn't get far. The National Guardsmen broke from their cover in the trees and charged us from every angle. Tear gas clawed at my eyes. All about me men, women and children screamed and sought to evade the clubs that swung at us indiscriminately. The Guardsmen on horses attempted to ride us down. Some fleeing marchers, running toward the fields, got tangled up in a barbed wire fence, where they continued to be clubbed. Near me Nat was trying to protect an elderly white lady. Two Guardsmen clubbed him into a ditch. I staggered about, half blinded by the tear gas. A blow caught me on the neck and I fell backwards, only to receive another blow as I was pitched toward the highway. I wrapped my arms tightly around my head to protect myself from the prancing hooves of the horses. When the screams of the women and children diminished a bit I thought it might be over. I stirred, only to see through my burning, tear-streaked eyes that the clubbing had moved to another section of the caravan.

I looked up. A guardsman stood over me. His uniform was torn and his cheek was bruised. Someone must have pulled him from his horse. Before I could protect my face again, his booted foot slammed into my right eye. His other foot followed, landing on my back and head. He kicked me as though he wanted to wipe me from the face of the earth. His hatred was obvious, worse than the detective on the train who had gone past hatred to a total indifference. He cursed me as he kicked. The world began to blacken and after a while I didn't feel anything anymore.

I had now experienced the power of the State. I realized that if the National Guardsmen had been told to shoot us down like dogs, we would have been shot down like dogs. Opposed by such power, what could we really do to change our condition? This question was depressing.

The 1932 election campaign had heated up. President Hoover continued to promise a chicken in every pot and a car in every garage. Franklin D. Roosevelt promised "a new deal," and most of the major newspapers had become hysterical in their attempt to brand him a communist.

In those states where Black people could vote, they came out to cast their ballots for Roosevelt. So did the unemployed, the union people, the small businessmen and the farmers. When Roosevelt won by a landslide there was tremendous rejoicing.

Black folks went wild. People danced in the soup kitchens and the unemployment lines. Nat, Jim Roberson and I joined a lot of other folks and went from one rent party to another. There was a celebration going on at the office of the South Side Tenant's Council where we stopped by and said hello to Oliver Law. He asked me how my eye was and I told him it was okay, except that it watered slightly when the wind blew. He never mentioned anything about how he had also been beaten. Everyone wanted to talk to him, get close to him. He came out of the hospital several times more popular than before.

President Roosevelt pushed through the Wagner Act, giving workers the right to organize unions without interference from their employers. Immediately after I was hired as a relief waiter by the Pennsylvania Railroad I started talking to the waiters about forming a union. Our working conditions were deplorable and our pay low. We were completely at the company's mercy. We had to change that, because if we didn't, who would? Furthermore, why shouldn't we have Black stewards in charge of some of the diners? I was amazed at my own persuasiveness. The younger waiters were very receptive. I began dreaming of organizing unions all over the country. However, the older waiters balked and were suspicious. A union to them meant the American Federation of Labor, which had a history of discrimination against Blacks. They argued, "Why should we join a union that might turn out like the AFL?"

I had trouble convincing them that the Congress of Industrial Organizations (CIO), the new labor union that was struggling to build membership, would not discriminate and that maybe we could affiliate with them, or maybe we could go independent as A. Phillip Randolph's Pullman Porters were thinking of doing. The older men remained doubtful.

A breakthrough finally came when I replaced a waiter for one trip on a dining car. There was not a man on it who had less than twenty years' service. We had finished serving dinner by the time we reached Lima, Ohio, giving me plenty of time to talk union before arriving in Pittsburgh, Pennsylvania.

The bull session started about the union. I argued all that I knew about unions. The white stewards had their union, but on this night the steward sat on the other side of the diner. I had no idea he was overhearing the argument about unions. All of a sudden he came in, entered the argument and took my side. The next morning, Mason, a thirty-year man, said to me, "Yates, I have been with this man (meaning the steward) for twenty years. You have done something that has never been done before. You got our steward to discuss something with the crew, outside of working duties." This was my breakthrough. I began to organize, both old and young.

I soon organized a meeting at the Pullman Porters Union Hall in South Michigan. One hundred men came with their union cards. I already was labelled by the railroad company as an "agitator," and since I had very little seniority I simply found myself not being called for jobs anymore. I warmed the bench in the "bull pen," growing desperate for a job again. My situation seemed even worse now, if no more than because there was so much promise in the air, a new President, my new friends, my hope for organizing a union, and occasional closeness between Bessie and me, but I was still unemployed. What had changed? Nothing. I was right back where I started.

Some things were not the same anymore. Tension between Bessie and me was at the breaking point. Suppose those rumors I heard that waiters were being hired in New York were true? I would not be known as an agitator for the union there. The whole idea of leaving Chicago was tearing my heart to bits, but it couldn't be any other way.

"Now", I said, "I must talk to somebody, maybe my friend Frank". I trudged my way through the deep snow until I reached State Street and then turned south to Fifty-fifth Street. I told my whole story to Frank. He was rather shocked when I told him I might be leaving Chicago soon. He gave me no encouragement. In fact, he was very much against the idea of my leaving Chicago. When I left him I was more or less positive I wouldn't be going to New York. But on my way home I met a young man called Lester Arnold. We had once worked part-time together, washing dishes at one of the Chicago speakeasies on Rush Street, just north of the Loop. He, too, was jobless. The first thing he said to me was, "I want to leave this doggone town."

"What about New York?" I asked.

"Anywhere but Chicago."

I went home to pack. Bessie and I talked about it. She didn't like my decision, but I had to go.

Chapter 5

New York

During the early spring of 1935 Lester and I found ourselves lying in a ditch alongside the railroad tracks, along with hundreds of other hobos, on Chicago's far South Side. We warmed our hands over a fire built inside huge tin cans and waited for a freight train that would take us to New York City. Eventually some freight trains rumbled by, and we hopped one. We looked forward to our destination and to brighter employment prospects.

Halfway between Chicago and New York small signs with a tiny golden chicken on them appeared, announcing in even smaller letters "Only 5 cents." As the signs became more frequent, the chickens grew larger. All the hobos on the train stared in disbelief. A chicken dinner cost sixty cents, and more often you would only get a quarter of a chicken. How could anyone be selling an entire chicken for five cents? We were all tempted to disregard the billboards but they were so numerous we couldn't. After a time the signs were even lit up with brilliant lights illuminating a giant-sized chicken.

Lester ceased sipping from his bottle and started blinking at the bright neon lights.

"Well, maybe the closer we come to New York the cheaper everything gets."

"But five cents? You can't hardly buy the neck of a chicken for that."

"Well, I don't know," Lester said. "I been telling you, New York ain't Chicago. It's the World Capital! We been trapped there in Chicago where there ain't no jobs, where ain't nothing happening any more. We shoulda took off a long time ago. I mean, man, in New York even chicken is cheaper!"

I didn't say anything. I started believing in those signs, too. All the hobos were acting nervous. Some pretended they weren't watching the signs, but they were. I got the impression they meant to jump off the train the minute the train pulled through the town where the chicken was sold so cheaply. They were tensed up and ready to outrun each other to get to the chicken first. I saw Lester stealing a glance at the hobos filling the boxcar, as though he was worried there would not be enough chicken for everyone.

The engine far up ahead whistled several times and pulled into the town of the cheap chicken. It was either the State of New Jersey or New York, perhaps less than a hundred miles from New York City. The sign of the golden chicken had become gigantic now. It dwarfed the old election posters of Franklin D. Roosevelt, with his fatherly smile, of Herbert Hoover, with his finger pointing to a new car in a garage. An arrow pointed toward a building on top of a hill where the chicken was supposedly sold.

Six hobos had leapt from the train and were running for the hill before Lester could get set to move. Then he glanced at me anxiously. "C'mon! Man, we gonna lose out!" My mouth felt dry, my stomach empty. I had only one dollar left between me and the world out there. All I could see was chicken, "Five-cent chicken," along the railway.

I plunged off the train after Lester, calculating that even after I bought the chicken for five cents, I'd have ninety-five cents left with which to tackle New York. As I charged up the hill with Lester, trying to overtake the other hobos, I thought it might be wise to buy three or four chickens. Then I would be sure of eating for at least a week while I looked for work.

Men stumbled and fell over each other. A short, skinny man went down in front of us, but kept crawling until he got to his feet again. We veered around him. I was amazed at Lester's speed. He seemed to have become completely sober. Only one man was ahead of us now, but he was so exhausted he had to grasp the restaurant door and catch his breath. Lester and I burst into the restaurant. The smell of food was all around us. A few customers sat at the counter eating hot dogs, sauerkraut, chili and beans. Breathlessly, we hurried toward the waitress and ordered chicken. "Chicken!" we demanded. "Five-cent chicken, please!" The waitress didn't even blink, though she seemed to wear a sad smile. From behind the counter she gave us a small, neatly wrapped cellophane package. We stared at the red, white and blue ribbons. The men behind us craned their necks to see what we had. "Naw," Lester said hoarsely. "We want the chicken."

"That's it," the waitress said.

We gazed at it again. Inside the cellophane was a miniature chocolate bar designed to resemble a chicken. "That's it?" Lester asked numbly.

"That's all. Unless you want hot dogs and chili. The sauerkraut is good, too."

"Well," Lester mumbled incoherently. He was so bewildered he pulled out ten cents and paid for two chocolate bars. We went out, passing the long line of men which stretched beyond the door and halfway down the hill. We found a grassy spot under a tree, plopped down and sat there staring at our chicken. The freight train, long gone, had left us behind. How could we get to New York now? "Any fool ought to know you can't buy no chicken for five cents!" Lester moaned furiously.

"Don't look at me. You were one of the first to jump off the train."

After swallowing our chicken dinners in one gulp, the two of us started hiking up the road. We found that we were somewhere in the eastern part of New Jersey and quite close to New York. We soon reached the city of Newark. Lester could not quite figure out the spelling and insisted that we were in New York City. That reminded me of the time I worked as a dining car waiter and heard older men talk about train adventures during the early twenties, when thousands of Blacks migrated North to the major cities. When the trains approached Newark, the last stop before New York City, the train conductor would shout his usual station call, "Newark, Newark!" The train would then empty because people thought they had arrived in New York. But the story was not so innocent. Certain political powers would tip the conductors to purposely deceive the migrant southern Blacks, and in that way Newark became their destination instead of New York.

When we finally arrived in New York City, we didn't see the Empire State building nor did we get to Harlem. Somewhere around Canal Street we came across a soup line and we joined it. There we were told where we could find a cheap room for the night.

It was a flophouse with rows and rows of beds that creaked with tossing, snoring and groaning men. In the middle of that night I thought someone had set me on fire. I turned and tossed nightmarishly on the narrow cot, feeling like I was burning alive. I felt like orphans must have felt, who had been burned to death during the draft riots of the Civil War. Poor whites had blamed Blacks for having to go fight in the war and had set a hospital ablaze with Black children in it.

I heard Lester groaning loudly. He seemed to be having a nightmare, too. I struck a match. Bedbugs, bloated with blood, scurried away from the light. My body was nearly covered with the horrible, blood-sucking creatures. I jumped up, yelling and beating them off me. Lester sprang up, too. Frantically we brushed the bugs back off the bed and onto the floor. Most of the other men only stirred briefly and then fell back into their tormented sleep.

Lester and I stumbled away from the place. We walked through the nocturnal New York streets until we found a park where we slept among other men. Early in the morning two policemen came by and smashed us on the bottoms of our feet with their nightsticks. We sat up howling in pain and grabbing our feet. The policemen didn't even look back as they walked away. Tears swelled in Lester's eyes. "How come I let you talk me into coming to a crazy town like this?"

■ ■ ■

"Hey!" someone shouted and continued, "What's your name?" I was not aware who this stranger was talking to, so I ignored him.

My blurred mind registered that I was sitting somewhere in a park, the place where I sometimes came to sleep now that I couldn't pay rent and had lost my room. During the day there were speakers in the park, much like it had been in Washington Park in Chicago. Through a wine-induced haze, the words of the speakers occasionally succeeded in reaching me. "Defend Angelo Herndon!" "Down with Hitler and Mussolini!" " Down with Capitalists!" " End discrimination against Negroes and Jews!"

A white man and a Black man stood before me. The Black one shook my shoulder, "Comrade, what's your name?" The white man pushed his fist angrily into his hand. "Too far gone," he said, referring to me. The Black man was angered by what his friend just said. I was also angry. I looked around at all the other men in the park and felt I could still hold my head up with pride.

"I saw him reading Du Bois just the other day," the Black one said. "If he was sober enough to read, he ought to be sober enough to learn." I felt I should explain, defend myself in some way, but I said nothing and they resumed their conversation. "Too late," the white man replied sadly. "We're losing thousands every day. Millions sinking into despair. Can't shake their bourgeois dreams fast enough."

"What's your name?" the Black man insisted.

"What?" I finally murmured.

"Your name!"

"James. James Yates."

"Listen, Jimmy. Get a hold of yourself. The other day I saw you reading Du Bois. What happened to your book?"

"I don't know. Lost it."

"Come with us. Have some soup."

I got up and they walked me between them. In the distance I could hear some speakers hotly debating. My newfound Black friend said, "My name is Alonzo. Alonzo Watson. And this is Comrade Herman Wolfowitz."

I mumbled "hello." I saw that we were leaving Union Square Park. We crossed the street to a restaurant and Herman went to the counter and brought back three bowls of pea soup.

Alonzo was in his early twenties, of medium build and rather quiet in manner. He asked me, "What other writers have you read?"

"Not many others, except Langston Hughes, but I've been trying to read Karl Marx."

Alonzo looked at Comrade Herman. "You see? I thought he had something. If a man reads, he can find his way." He looked at me again. "I'm unemployed, too. Millions of people are without work all over the world, but you don't let yourself go. You've got to keep fighting. You ever been politically active?"

"What?"

"Politically active . . . you know, demonstrations, strikes, things like that . . ."

"Oh, well, in Chicago, I started to organize the railroad dining car waiters and I was in the march to Springfield."

"Springfield! That's terrific!" Alonzo was pleased to hear that. He glanced at Herman. "You see? Sometimes we judge too quickly, too harshly." He regarded me once more. "A good friend of mine was in jail and beaten for helping to organize that march."

"Oliver Law?"

Herman stared at me skeptically. "You know Oliver?"

I bragged a little. "I met him several times in Washington Park. He had an eviction attempt stopped on my friend's apartment."

"You see?" Alonzo said ecstatically. "You see? He knows Oliver."

"And Richard Wright," I rushed on, "James Roberson and Nat Dickson."

"Damn! and how is old crazy Nat? And I hear Dick is writing a novel."

"He sure is. He was with us, too, on that march to Springfield."

We talked a few more minutes but my mind began to wander. The need of a job and a room for the night kept distracting me. I said good-bye to my first New York acquaintances. I told them I would see them soon again in Union Square Park.

A few days later as I walked along Fourteenth Street and passed by the many decorated windows, I saw Easter bonnets and was reminded that Easter was only a week away. Walking away from the fancy windows my thoughts turned to my two children in Chicago. If only I had the money, I thought sadly, I could send them gifts for Easter. Knowing that around Eastertime extra help is needed on railroad dining cars, I set out for Pennsylvania Station to apply for a job. I carried my small suitcase which held all of my belongings including my waiter's uniform.

At the station I was given directions to the dining car department which was located in Sunnyside, Queens. When I arrived there were only a few men lined up in front of the office. Soon it was my turn to be interviewed. I was asked whether I had dining room experience, then I was given an application to fill out. Only a few minutes after returning the form I was told to report for work the next morning.

I thanked the interviewer and walked away thinking about how I might celebrate having gotten a few days of work. I decided, with one dollar in my pocket, to make my first visit to Harlem. I had been told about Father Divine's restaurant where one could get a meal for fifteen cents.

After eating dinner, I still had enough money to spend the evening at the Savoy Ballroom on Lenox Avenue. As I walked along the avenues of Harlem, the same ones my uncle had walked years before me, I thought about his letter to my father in which he explained about waiting for a ship that would take him to Africa. My Uncle was one of the thousands of Blacks in the Marcus Garvey Back-to-Africa Movement.

It is a small world we live in, just a block away from the Savoy, I stopped dead in my tracks. In front of me stood my old roommate from Chicago, Johnny McGowan. I forgot all about Marcus Garvey and the Savoy.

We embraced warmly. Before I could think, I was telling him the story of how I had spent three hours in the subway trying to find my way to Harlem. He laughed. I began to feel good.

Like myself, Johnny was unemployed. Being almost flat broke we skipped the Savoy and spent the night talking as we roamed the streets of Harlem until long after midnight. Harlem sparked my imagination far more than Chicago or anyplace I had ever been. I wondered if people ever went to sleep. We passed the crowds pouring out of the late, late show at the Apollo on 125th Street and those at Small's Paradise on Seventh Avenue. Eating places seemed to fill up only after four in the morning, the closing hour at the Savoy Ballroom which was the jewel and pride of Harlem. In fact, it was the Mecca for New York City as a whole. Two big bands played nightly. Imagine Duke Ellington, Cab Calloway and the legendary bands of the era.

With only a few hours of sleep I made my way to the railroad yards at Sunnyside, Queens. It was the Sunday before Easter and I was starting another stint as a dining car waiter. This train traveled west to Pittsburgh. There the dining car was sidetracked to the great railroad yards east of Pittsburgh. We spent five days there before returning to New York at night. This meant we received no travel pay. Our regular pay was a munificent twenty-three cents an hour, so it was easy to understand why most dining car workers wanted to join a union.

Easter was over and so was this job, but I was told to hang around in case there was another opening. For three weeks I sat in the bullpen. I assumed my old organizing role, applying the skills that I had learned in Chicago where I had also worked for the Pennsylvania Railroad. I had thought things were bad in the western division, but that paled in comparison to what I was finding in the East. I wondered how much worse things could be.

I did get one job that was a two-day trip to Washington, D.C. The trip was rigged so that at the end of the run I received a check on payday for fifty cents. I wanted to frame it for organizing purposes, but I couldn't afford to. During this year of 1935, George Brown became the first president of the Dining Car Employees Union, Local 370. I was more than proud as I became the first man among the dining car workers to sign a union card.

After the union was formed the workers got a contract signed by the bosses. The waiters and cooks who didn't want to sleep on the small cots in the dining car, now could sleep in the Pullman car like the white stewards. Workers also won a pay raise, and a guarantee of time off each month so they could visit their families.

I was very happy about the growth of the union, and wanted to tell my friends in Union Square about it. One day in early summer I made my way to the park and walked to its north end. Herman Wolfowitz was standing on a park bench, speaking to a crowd on the danger of the rise of fascism in Europe. We Blacks had our own fascism to contend with. The Ku Kluxers and lynchers here at home were an ever-present threat. While Herman spoke, I saw myself as a boy seeing five men and four women dangling from a bridge—lynched.

Before Herman finished speaking, Alonzo Watson arrived. The three of us then chatted about what we had been up to, and Herman offered to let me stay at his place. I accepted the offer and soon moved to his loft on West Twelfth Street where Alonzo also lived. It was not far from the Albert Hotel. Herman slept in the front part of the loft and Alonzo and I shared the room in the rear. I was surprised to find out that both Herman and Alonzo were artists, Herman a sculptor, and Alonzo, a painter. The three of us shared food and kept the place clean. We did our cooking on an electric hotplate. It was agreed that when I found a job I'd help pay the rent. I became a part of the family of three.

Outside in the neighborhood we often encountered hostility. White people stared at Alonzo and me, wondering what we were doing in the area. Like most New York hotels, the Hotel Albert, where famous people stayed, didn't admit Blacks, although Greenwich Village, ironically, before the turn of the century, had been a section of the city with a large Black population. High rents and discrimination had driven the Blacks further north, eventually to Harlem.

During 1935-36 Alonzo and I were very much involved in the struggle to free Angelo Herndon from his sentence of eighteen to twenty years on a Georgia chain gang. Angelo's case was the Dred Scott issue of the 1930's. A world-wide campaign was launched to release him from prison.

Angelo Herndon was a young labor organizer who worked with Black miners and sharecroppers. During 1932 literally thousands of families had been dropped from the relief rolls in Georgia. For having led a demonstration in Atlanta, Angelo was arrested on an old insurrection charge, a state law that dated back to the Reconstruction era. He was convicted and sentenced to eighteen years in prison. Eventually a higher court reversed the verdict, but the State Supreme Court upheld it. Finally, due to mounting support, in 1937 the US Supreme Court held that he was indeed convicted wrongfully.

■ ■ ■

It wasn't long before I got a part-time job with the WPA: that is, Alonzo and Herman got it for me. Some of their comrades who worked in the WPA office finagled jobs for all three of us. I was dispatched to the West Side Highway where I dug up old bricks and laid down new ones. Asphalt was not widely used and bricks and cobblestones lined the highway as far as the eye could see. I was so happy, I wrote Bessie a five-page letter and I sent my father a batch of postcards, one with a picture of the Empire State Building on it. I tried to save money, though I wasn't making that much. I familiarized myself with the streets of Harlem, keeping a sharp eye open for a cheap apartment.

Some Saturday nights Alonzo and I would make a beeline for Harlem and let off some steam. We joined the swinging and swaying crowd of Black as well as white folks at the Savoy Ballroom, the "home of happy feet." The big bands were coming into vogue and we danced until the crack of dawn. The Cotton Club was located in Harlem, too, as were other ritzy clubs, but they mostly catered to whites, though they had Black name entertainers. Alonzo and I stared angrily at the limousines and Rolls Royces lining the curbs in front of these clubs, but knew better than to seek admittance. We simply wouldn't have been welcome.

Occasionally, out of old habit, I went to church, mostly to the Abyssinian Baptist Church where Adam Clayton Powell often preached. One morning he preached about living now, rather than dying and going to heaven later. I sat there among the sisters and brothers attired in their best Sunday clothes and listened to the choir singing "Going to Lay My Burden Down" and other favorites of my mother, and nearly cried from nostalgia. What would my family be doing now? Mama, Papa, Grandmama, and my two sisters? I longed to see them and thought once I got organized in New York I could send for them. My train of thought was broken by the fiery sermon of young Powell and I rocked and clapped along with the others in the church.

"Is it right, in the eyes of God, for white people to own stores in our own community, and not employ a single one of our young people as clerks? Is it right, in the eyes of God, for white people to come to Harlem, to swarm all over Harlem seeking to amuse themselves in clubs that slammed their doors upon Black faces? Is it right that we don't have jobs, are barred from the city's hotels, are denied the best in medical facilities?"

"Amen!" the people shouted. "Preach!"

"Maybe Blacks should organize picket lines before the clubs and hospitals and hotels that won't admit them. . . ."

"Yes! Yes! Preach!"

"We're not going to the river and lay our burdens down. We're going to look upon our shoulders and dump the burdensome white man off our backs."

"Amen!"

I left the church in a state of agitation. Powell was saying some of the same things the comrades were saying in a more scientific and theoretical way, but Powell's emotion, coupled with the atmosphere of the church, caused something to really hit home inside my soul. I walked toward the subway at 125th Street, wondering how I could accelerate my activities to change the rotten conditions in

the world. At one street corner a mass of people surrounded a speaker who was lecturing a crowd from a
stepladder. I figured it was Marcus Garvey's people or one
of the splinter nationalist groups. I had acquaintances in
most of the other movements, but I already decided, perhaps like Professor Blakeney, that the solution to the Black
problem was not to go back to Africa but to force democracy to work here in America. I skirted the mass of people.
A strange anger pulsated in them. An electric feeling per-
vaded the air, not only coming from the people but out of
the bowels of Harlem itself. More cops than usual
patrolled the streets. I stopped a man hurrying toward the
rally and asked him what was happening.

"Why, man, don't you know?" I said I didn't.

"That Mussolini has invaded the homeland of
Ethiopia!"

It was the first week of October 1935, and things were
moving fast. The Depression continued while Hitler pro-
ceeded to consolidate his power in Germany. The world
was tense and New York was alive with energy.

■ ■ ■

One day Alonzo and I went to Union Square Park to
pass out leaflets for what would be one of the largest
political rallies I had ever witnessed. It was held at Madison
Square Garden; the noted scholar W.E.B. Du Bois was
moderator. I had read Du Bois's book *Black Reconstruction* and its sequel *Propaganda of History*. The latter is a
bitter indictment of the "whites only" American history
establishment. Although I had never attended a university,
this Du Bois critique was very real to me. In 1910 Du Bois
had quit Atlanta University to take on the editor's job at
The Crisis, the new publication of the NAACP, the National
Association for Advancement of Colored People.

The rally was sponsored by the League Against War
and Fascism. Mr. W.E.B. Du Bois was the chairman of the

meeting. The roster of speakers was a "Who's Who" of American justice and freedom fighters. Among the first to speak was Vito Marcantonio, a progressive leader of Harlem's east side, the twentieth Congressional District. Born into a traditional Italian family, Marcantonia was a protege of Mayor Fiorello LaGuardia, and had established himself as a leader of the New York American Labor Party. A former congressman, he played a leading role in electing Blacks to the state and local legislatures.

I knew very little about the next man called to the rostrum, but I knew I was in the presence of greatness when I heard Paul Robeson, a man known everywhere around the world except in his own country. An all-American football player while a student at Rutgers University, then a law student at Columbia University, Robeson spoke half a dozen languages fluently. In the role of Othello with a major Shakespearean theatrical company in London he not only launched a spectacular stage career, he smashed the color barrier for all time. In his own country racism delayed his debut in such a role for fifteen more years.

On this evening, he moved the crowd to frenzy by singing "The Minstrel Boy," "Shenandoah," "Let My People Go" and "Old Man River."

Another speaker that moved the audience was A. Phillip Randolph. President of the Black Brotherhood of Sleeping Car Porters union, he represented the aggressive left wing of the American Federation of Labor. In 1936 he was elected President of the National Negro Congress. He spoke this evening on the status of the Negro in industry, politics and education. He expressed indignation over the invasion of Ethiopia by Mussolini's armies. He linked the cruel, uncalled-for rape of Ethiopia to the terrible repression of Black people in the United States.

As I listened I thought how my own life had been changed because of this man. His Brotherhood of Sleeping Car Porters union had in a broad sense showed us the way when we first attempted to organize dining car workers.

They also gave us practical aid by allowing us to use their meeting hall. Here he was before me, Phillip Randolph, a man who gave so much of his life for freedom of the working people. At the conclusion of the demonstration, a collection was taken for the League Against War and Fascism. Thousands of dollars were raised that evening. As we were leaving I began to read one of the small pamphlets distributed at the rally, explaining the true nature of Hitler's and Mussolini's desire to conquer the world. When it came to what Hitler said about the approaching fight between Joe Louis and Max Schmeling, I recognized the same racist theories that Senator Bilbo of Mississippi exposed about Black folks being inferior.

I turned to Alonzo and Herman to show them what Hitler said about Joe Lewis, essentially that Black folks have no brains. Alonzo added, "I bet Joe Lewis will knock the hell out of Schmeling!"

I recall the celebrations in Harlem the night that Joe Lewis beat "pure-race" Max Schmeling. Thousands of Harlemites representing many organizations, including the Harlem Communist organizations, paraded behind banners reading: "Louis Up - Hitler Down," "Drive Race Hatred out of Town," "Aryan Supremacy Taboo", "Louis KO's Fascism," "Ethiopia Fight On."

As Mussolini's massive attack against Ethiopia continued we focused all of our energy into stopping the fascists. We roamed the city collecting food and clothing to be sent to the victims of the bombs. In addition to passing out leaflets denouncing the war we gathered signatures and sent them to President Roosevelt, entreating him to stop Mussolini.

■ ■ ■

A whole new crisis emerged with which we were forced to deal. Stores owned by Italians were being looted by a minority of misguided Blacks. In an attempt to prevent this from spreading, we printed a leaflet explaining that many Italians were against Mussolini's invasion of Ethiopia and pointing out that throughout Italy people were demonstrating against the war. The proof that we were correct in our statement came later when the Italian Army was sent to Spain and hundreds of Italians volunteered to join the International Brigade, and to fight against the army. Most Blacks saw the war in Ethiopia as merely another malicious attempt by whites to destroy Blacks. The Garvey people and other nationalist groups played well on these feelings. Sometimes it was difficult to quiet a Black audience long enough to speak.

We heard that the same sort of thinking prevailed across the country. Blacks in every large city—Chicago, Detroit, Los Angles, Boston and New York—were rioting. The police were out in force and the National Guard was alerted. Alonzo helped to organize much of the defense work, including those who wanted to fight in Ethiopia.

Suddenly it was too late. Ethiopia had been defeated by Mussolini's troops and modern air force. The League of Nations looked the other way while Haile Selassie fled into exile and another piece of Africa was colonized. The date was May 2, 1936, scarcely ten weeks before the Spanish fascist's rebellion.

For several days Alonzo wouldn't speak to anyone, and no one dared to speak to him. I worried about Alonzo so much that I had no time to think about myself. Herman, too, gingerly moved around Alonzo with caution, avoiding any pretext for an argument. Alonzo flung himself back into his paintings, and more canvasses appeared with sightless eyes and broken limbs—canvasses that he seemed to reject as fast as he painted them. He was happier when he did posters of giant fists raised in the air.

I slept around the clock, giddy with exhaustion. I tried not to feel like the bottom was falling out of the world again. I attempted vainly to amuse Alonzo. The loft had become a very gloomy place.

Then one day Herman rushed in with an armful of groceries and newspapers. He held five different papers in his hands and all of them read, in effect: "Republican Spain Under Attack!"

The headlines screamed out at us and the fascist collaboration in Spain seemed to jump off the pages. One paper boldly announced: "Mussolini Pledges the Support of His Troops," then the article went on, "seasoned by their conquest of Ethiopia, to the cause of the fascist generals in Spain . . . Adolph Hitler has also offered his support to the . . ."

The article concluded by saying that the Spanish Republican government, democratically elected, was asking the entire world for volunteers to come to Spain and aid in its fight against Mussolini, Hitler and the fascist generals.

Herman shouted, at no one in particular, "Now you see? What did I tell you? I've been saying for three years that Hitler would move. First he'd tighten his Nazi grip on Germany and then he'd look around at the rest of Europe. Such a maniac cannot be appeased. I've said it over and over. But who would listen?"

Alonzo didn't look up. He stared silently at his paper. Then he said in his typical quiet manner, "I'm going. I'm volunteering. The time for talking is over. You've got to put your conviction where your mouth is!"

Herman was startled for a moment. He went to his unfinished canvas and touched it absently. I was silent also, with the question pressing upon me, "Am I prepared to go to Spain with Alonzo?" I had been more than ready to go to Ethiopia, but that was different. Ethiopia, a Black nation, was part of me. I was just beginning to learn about the reality of Spain and Europe, but I knew what was at stake. There the poor, the peasants, the workers and the unions, the socialists and the communists, together had won an election against the big landowners, the monarchy and the right-wingers in the military. It was the kind of victory that would have brought Black people to the top levels of government if such an election had been won in the USA. A Black man would be Governor of Mississippi. The new government in Spain was dividing its wealth with the peasants. Unions were organizing in each factory and social services were being introduced. Spain was the perfect example for the world I dreamed of.

Now all of it was about to be wiped out. The former rulers were determined to retake power. They were being supported by fascists all over the world, including, I was sure, many in the United States. How could I not volunteer?

I stood up in agitation. I needed to be alone for a moment.

I needed time to think, so I walked away from Alonzo and Herman and went into the back of the loft. I stood before a big window that gave me a full view of Thirteenth Street. There was a crowd of people moving along the sidewalk, and automobiles blowing their horns. Somehow I didn't see or hear a thing, my thoughts were all about Spain. I pictured Hitler applauding the lynching of Blacks in America, and I visualized Mussolini raping Ethiopia, the only independent Black country. What would things be like in the US with a Hitler and with Bilbo as his lieutenant? I realized that if the fascists were not defeated in Spain, a bigger war would surely come soon. I said to myself, "My mind is made up, I will go to Spain!"

When I returned, Alonzo and Herman were talking.

"The arrogance! The audacity!" Alonzo was saying indignantly. "Using his goddamn troops to practice on colored people, now sending them to Spain!"

"Color, color!" Herman added. "It's not a question of color. It's profit and territory. Mark my word! Mussolini may send troops and supplies to General Franco, but the fascists' battle is going to be won in Spain, if we allow it, not by Mussolini but by Hitler."

"What did you decide?" I asked Herman.

"About what?"

"Are you volunteering?"

"Was there ever any doubt? Alonzo and I are signing up tomorrow."

"And you?" Alonzo asked. He watched me hopefully.

"Well, that makes three of us, tomorrow."

The year of 1936 was pivotal for all of us. In the North, half of our families were on relief, while in the South, white mobs continued to lynch at least one Black every three weeks. During this time the NAACP was forced to withdraw its support from President Roosevelt when he refused to give his practical support to their anti-lynching bill and because not one piece of civil rights legislation had been proposed during his first term.

At the Berlin Olympics Jesse Owens won four gold medals, but down South we lost eight more lives to white lynch mobs. In the cities, North and South, thirty-six percent, more than one out of every three Black males, were unemployed. The average yearly income of rural southern Black families was $556, while for whites it was $1,535. In the northern cities the income of white families averaged $2,615, while for Blacks it was only $1,227.

The NAACP's magazine, *Crisis,* condemned the Republican Party's pledge of "protection" of the Black's economic status, stating: "This is precisely what the Negroes do not want . . . His present economic status is the chief cause of his discontent."

At the Democratic National Convention, South Carolina Senator "Cotton Ed" Smith walked out, vowing never to support "any political and social equality." The South Carolina delegation officially protested the presence of Blacks.

It is a sad indictment of American politics that the only political platform that seemed to recognize the reality of my life belonged to the Communist Party. Their platform stated: "The Negro people suffer doubly. Most exploited of working people, they are also the victims of Jim Crowism and lynchings. They are denied the right to live as human beings." In addition, the platform endorsed the "abolition of poll taxes and other limitations to the right to vote," and demanded the release of political prisoners like Tom Mooney, Angelo Herndon, and the Scottsboro boys. "We demand that the Negro people be guaranteed complete equality, equal rights to jobs, equal pay for equal work, the full right to organize, vote, serve on juries, and hold public office. Segregation and discrimination against Negroes must be declared a crime." It continued: "Heavy penalties must be established against mob rule, floggers and kidnappers, with the death penalty for lynchers. We demand the enforcement of the 13th, 14th and 15th amendments to the Constitution."

To a man like me, those words were heady stuff. Those who have difficulty understanding this have never walked in my shoes.

■ ■ ■

Alonzo and I went to apply for passports so we could go to Spain. Getting my passport was difficult because, as I mentioned at the beginning of my story, the State of Mississippi, in keeping with its Jim Crow policies, did not keep records of the birth of Black babies.

New reports from Spain on November 7, 1936, found the retreating Spanish Republic in a fierce battle against more than twenty-thousand Moroccans, Spanish legionnaires, and land supporters of the German and Italian fascist forces. The next morning it was reported that Madrid was under siege day and night. Orders had been given for citizens to build barricades. Masses of workers left for the front lines, many without weapons, ready to take up the rifles of the fallen.

Ironically, in this strong Catholic nation, women took part in the war. They built barricades, and a women's battalion fought before the Segovia Bridge.

I never will forget December 26, 1936. That night Alonzo, along with ninety-six other people, left for Spain. I was down at the dock and saw the boat pull away from the dock and make its way down the Hudson River and out into the open waters. Staring at the boat as it moved slowly out of sight, I couldn't accept the fact that I was not aboard. I began to imagine myself on the cold, black Atlantic in the vast darkness that separates each passenger from the others. I imagined that I was among the young thoughtful, anxious volunteers, black, brown and white—the best we have to offer.

Reality soon returned as I stood in the silence alone on the dock. I turned and headed back to the loft. The little room seemed empty. I stared at Alonzo's cot next to the window. I looked at the walls, bare except for an unfinished painting, and could almost see Alonzo standing with a paintbrush in his hand. I felt like the world had come to an end.

What should my next move be? The only things standing between me and Spain were my passport and the deep blue sea.

Chapter 6

Leaving for Spain

I paced the floor for hours wondering, how will I get to Spain? Then I stopped pacing and stood before the window staring into the dimly lighted street. I remembered how when my friend Allen was faced with the same problem, he had his mother sign an affidavit giving the exact date of his birth.

But my mother . . . I ruled that out. I could never let her know I was going to fight in a war. I decided to ask my first cousin, the one who nursed me when I was a baby, to assist me. I sent her an urgent letter saying I had a good job coming up and I needed an affidavit from her stating the date I was born—a little white lie. In a week I received the affidavit along with a letter which said how happy she was that I had found a job in these times.

On January 20, 1937, my passport in hand, I rushed across town to find out when the next boat would be leaving for Spain. To my surprise I was told that a new decision of the State Department had made it illegal for Americans to use their passport to enter Spain.

My thoughts returned to the night I stood on the dock watching the French liner "Normandie" depart with my friends. I didn't know it at the time, but along with Alonzo were four other Blacks—Walter Garland, Douglas Roach, Ed White and Oliver Law.

What was I to do? How could I get to Spain? I realized it was not necessary to go directly to Spain, that I could go to either England or France, then worry about getting to Spain. I selected France.

During the weeks in which I waited for my boat to leave, I read newspaper reports that said some Americans had participated in the battle to save Madrid. That was the battle of Jarama.

Finally, on February 20, 1937, I left New York aboard "Ile de France." Of the eight hundred passengers on board, about three hundred young men were headed for Spain, via France. All of our passports read "Not Valid for Spain."

The sea was stormy and at mealtimes the dining area was empty. I passed the time with one of my cabin mates, Herman Bottcher, who was also headed for Spain. During World War II, Bottcher would be awarded a field commission of captain in the United States Army for "extraordinary heroism and leadership in Battle." His courage and heroism made him one of the most highly acclaimed fighters in the Pacific theatre, where he died fighting in the South Pacific.

As we approached Le Havre, France, a loud voice boomed out over the ship's communication system calling out names from the passenger list—mine was the first name—and ordering us to go to a certain stateroom. By the time we were all assembled, there were almost three hundred young men in the room. A stout redheaded man from the United States consulate walked into the room and spoke bluntly. "I am aware you are headed for Spain, but now the French Government has closed the border." He went on to explain that if we were caught without money in France, we would be put in jail. Then he said, "You can return to the United States, at government expense, now. All who want to return, raise your hands."

From the crowded room only one hand was raised. To this day I believe that man was a plant. Nobody remembered seeing him on the boat during our journey.

The man from the consulate made us answer questions about what we planned on doing in France and how much money we had. We told him we were students visiting Germany, or Switzerland, or any place but Spain. He couldn't prove otherwise. He had asked me earlier how much money I had. I admitted having only three dollars, but added pointedly that I was expecting a money order of two hundred dollars from my family, waiting for me in Paris.

The French trainmen must have known we were being delayed on the boat, as they held the train until we were permitted to leave. Customs, knowing where we were headed, didn't search our baggage. Instead they rushed us along with a brisk salute.

As the train sped along to Paris, I realized that my seasickness had completely gone away. It must have been the same with the others for we all now made a beeline for the dining car. There I saw two Blacks that I had previously noticed on the boat. I didn't speak with them on the boat because I had been told not to talk with passengers other than my cabin mates. Now I said hello to one of them who identified himself as Vaughan Love and said he was from a little town called Dayton, Tennessee. I remembered that was the place of the famous Scopes Trial, in which Clarence Darrow defended the teaching of the theory of evolution in schools. The prosecution had been led by William Jennings Bryan. This trial was later portrayed in the drama "Inherit the Wind."

As Vaughan and I talked I saw his friend from the boat, another tall Black man. I asked, "Who's that entering the dining car?"

"Admiral Kilpatrick."

"No, I don't mean that white man."

"I know," Vaughan smiled. "I meant the Black man. That's the name on his passport."

"Admiral Kilpatrick! I never heard of a Black admiral."

"No," Vaughan laughed openly, "That's his birth name."

"Oh boy, Black people are really something. There must be some really interesting stories about how we get some of our names!"

We arrived in Paris about one o'clock in the morning. Arnold Reed was part of the delegation that greeted us. I knew him from New York and had the highest regard for this man who was later to die in Spain. Members of the French committee, which would be in complete charge of us while we were in France, escorted us to various hotels along the banks of the Seine River.

Although it was after midnight when we were all settled in our rooms, some of the men wanted to see a little of Paris and decided that there was no place better to go than the Chatelet Quarter of Paris. There the French enjoyed their late supper of onion soup at the famous marketplace. But, these guys were not looking for good soup. They had sex on their minds, as though this would be their last chance. In fact, for many, this turned out to be quite true. I didn't join the crowd that night, but two of us went to have a drink at a nearby cafe. I was no different from the others who had gone "hunting." I gawked at the beautiful French girls who sat sipping their drinks during the early morning hours. I thought they surely must be out for "business," not knowing that this was the way of life in Paris.

My hotel room overlooked the Seine. I shared a large room, formerly a suite, with an Englishman, a German, and a Swede, all volunteers waiting to enter Spain. From the window I watched the boats chug to and fro on the river. Further up the Seine was the Cathedral of Notre Dame.

I seldom remained in the room, because I enjoyed exploring Paris. Each day I fell more in love with the city. I walked along the Seine and looked at the bookstalls. I stood and watched the painters sketching the river and the people walking by. I thought of Herman Bottcher and wondered if he had been sent to Spain by boat.

I found the Champs Elysees and couldn't believe that I, a poor fellow from Mississippi, was walking upon such a famous street. It was here that the Black singer and dancer Josephine Baker sometimes strolled with her pet leopards, startling and exciting all of Paris. In contrast to the response I was accustomed to receiving from people in America, Parisians smiled and greeted me in the streets.

As I walked toward L'Arc de Triomphe, I paused before a terraced cafe. I wanted to stop for a cognac but suddenly lost my nerve. Would they serve me? With its gleaming white tablecloths, the cafe looked so rich and prosperous that I hesitated to enter. Suddenly the white faces of the people at the tables looked again like the American faces I'd known all my life.

Dejected, I turned and walked away and I began to sweat. The painful memories of being constantly rejected in my own country didn't allow me to risk entering a French cafe for fear of being turned away.

I slept fitfully that night, my feeling for Paris sullied. I woke up annoyed with myself. As friendly as the French people were in the streets and everywhere else, surely they wouldn't have refused to serve me at that cafe. I was allowing American racism to govern my conduct over here. I left the hotel determined to storm into the restaurant and demand to be served.

But the closer I got to the rich-looking cafe, the slower I walked. Instead of turning into the entrance, I kept on passing by, and my stomach churned as though I was going to vomit. My country had programmed me to accept the status of "nigger" and I just didn't know if I would ever be able to overcome it.

I circled the block and kept walking, still thinking I must eventually enter the cafe. I wished one of my roommates had come with me, but the Swede didn't speak

English and I didn't understand the German. I felt a bit uncomfortable around Kurt. It was difficult to believe that there were Germans who hated the Nazis as much, or even more, than I.

I only partly understood the Englishman. He spoke so properly I thought he should be in the movies. I was amazed to find that he was Jewish. I had thought that all Jewish people spoke like Jews in New York—like Herman. My roommate actually sounded like he was the King of England. I was learning so much about people, and the world, that sometimes I thought my head would split wide open. I knew I had to get over feeling like I was half a man.

I had walked so far away from the cafe that I became lost. I looked for the Champs Elysees. I became angry with myself. How in the hell was I going to face bullets in Spain when I couldn't face a cafe filled with French people?

I came upon the Place de la Concorde and continued walking in uncertainty; passing the prestigious Hotel Crillon, I spotted a Black man. It was the Admiral!

I stopped in surprise. He came out of the hotel and spoke to the uniformed doorman and then he went back in before I could call to him. I was astonished. Had some of the volunteers been put up in such a plush hotel? It seemed unlikely. What was Kilpatrick doing in that hotel? I headed uneasily for the entrance. If I hadn't seen the Admiral go in, without being thrown out, I'm sure I would have been too intimidated to enter the door.

My feet sank into the plush carpet and the chandeliers and mirrors were blinding. The air smelled of wealth and power. The people in such an elegant hotel couldn't be very sympathetic with the democratic government in Spain, I thought. They were privileged and surely intended to keep it that way.

The Admiral sat with his legs crossed in one of the forbidding-looking chairs. He had a newspaper before his dark face but apparently wasn't reading. His eyes popped wide open when he saw me. He jumped up and shook hands. Instantly his voice lowered itself to a whisper. "Don't tell me they put you up here?"

"No," I said. "Are you staying here?"

"No, no . . ." He hesitated. "Hell, I just stopped in to read the *Herald Tribune*." He looked around at people reflected in the mirrors. It was deadly quiet. "Let's get out of here."

Outside, he told the doorman, "Well, if Mr. Brown gets here, tell him I been here and gone."

"Very well, monsieur."

A half block up the street he burst out laughing. "I told him I was waiting for Mr. Brown to arrive before I checked in. But you know something? I could have checked in if I had the money. Yesterday I saw a Chinese and an African come in. No trouble. Bellhop grabbed their bags just like they did for everyone else. Sure, I know France is a colonial country. But here in Paris they don't rush to tell you if you're Black, get back."

I was laughing, too. "Maybe the doorman thought I was Mr. Brown." We cracked up anew over the absurd effects of racism.

I was embarrassed, and somewhat reluctantly I told him about the cafe I had been hesitant about entering.

He adjusted the beret he now sported. "Let's go check it out, it's time we find out how the enemy's been living."

At the cafe we were seated with bows and "Oui, monsieur." We ordered our drinks, sat back and enjoyed watching the people. That same evening we were told to prepare to leave Paris early next morning.

At six o'clock in the morning we left Paris. All of the volunteers that stayed in the same hotel climbed into buses which took us to the train station. From there a train carrying three hundred volunteers took us to Arles in southern France, only a few miles from the Spanish border.

As the train pulled into the station at Arles, I could hear a band playing. The volunteers were led by the band as we marched out of the station in four columns and down the main street of the town. Next came the mayor and then the entire city council. Arles was one of the many towns in France which had a communist mayor at that time.

■ ■ ■

For two weeks we waited for orders to move. Our French allies, who would give us the signal to go, were waiting for weakness in the line of defense along the border dividing Spain and France. French soldiers, who had been ordered to respect the embargo against Spain, patrolled the border. Our leaders had some vague hope they might be able to smuggle us across the border and that we wouldn't have to make the long climb over the mountain. Gradually we all began to realize we would have to make the climb.

Gunal, the Englishman with whom I had shared a room in Paris, continued doing push-ups and knee-bends throughout the trip. In Paris he had waited politely each morning until the rest of us were awake before clearing the area next to his bed and exercising. He was about ten years older than most of us. He was short, with a full round chest and stomach which heaved with tension each time he climbed the hotel stairs. On the train he kept to himself and continued his exercises. Now, in Arles, he barely slept. A haunted look had come to his eyes and a growing desperation now characterized his exercises. Still, he never complained about the prospects of climbing the Pyrenees mountains.

■ ■ ■

One evening before sundown we boarded buses for Montille. The atmosphere was hush-hush. Fascist spies and sympathizers could be watching our movements. At

Montille we were immediately hustled into a fleet of cars. We sped down the straightest road I had ever traveled, shaded by unending rows of trees on either side. Looking ahead it seemed like one long gleaming arrow pointing me to my destination—Spain. About five miles before we were to arrive, the driver noticed that we were being followed. He told us it was the border patrol. His foot went down on the accelerator, but the big limousine which was carrying fifteen of us, weighed too much to shake our pursuers. He stopped suddenly and told us to make a run for it into the surrounding wooded area. We stayed hidden in the trees for what must have been about a half hour, then we began to see other men coming into the woods. To our relief we realized that they had come to join us. The driver had been mistaken. The car that was following us was part of the fleet of cars bringing more volunteers from Arles.

Out of nowhere two Spanish guides showed up and led us slowly, inch by inch, through the woods until we eventually came into sight of the road which marked the border.

I could see the border patrol. We were all being so quiet that it was possible to actually hear the footsteps of the guards. Suddenly, I lifted my eyes above the trees and there I saw the Pyrenees mountains looming massively and forbiddingly against the greyish sky. My eyes returned to the patrols. Two passed each other, continuing to walk in opposite directions. It was so strange. With three hundred men in the woods, they must have sensed us. If they did, they never turned back. It was almost as if they knew. The Spanish guides ordered us to cross the road. I will always believe that the French border patrols must have been sympathetic to the cause of Spain.

I was awed by the silence but felt secure in the presence of the hundreds of comrades marching with me. At last I was on my way! Nothing but a mountain separated me from the war. I would soon see my buddy Alonzo, and probably Herman, Vaughan Love, and the Admiral. We would win this war. How could we lose? We would win because we were on the right side, we were on the side of the poor and the oppressed people.

I wondered if Alonzo had been in the front lines at Jarama in the battle to save Madrid. The capitalist newspapers painted the war as though we were losing. Several times they had eagerly reported that Madrid had fallen to Generalissimo Franco and Mussolini's troops, when it hadn't. They were aware that a quick fascist victory would obscure the one-sided nature of the embargo. While men, war materials and even medical supplies were being denied the Republicans, French and English capitalists were not only lending the fascists moral support, but supplying them with guns, planes and tanks. The fascists, including Hitler Germany, received oil from the United States, and in particular from the large oil companies. Without that support they could not maintain their huge war machines. I didn't believe the newspapers. I knew from the experience of our march to Springfield just how falsely events were reported. Madrid would not fall. Republican Spain would not fall. We would go on to create other Republican states throughout the world. Perhaps even in Mississippi!

As I looked up from the bottom of the Pyrenees mountains to their endless rise into the sky, I couldn't help but feel a bit apprehensive. How would we ever be able to scale them? It was dark except for a faint sliver of moonlight. Suppose one lost his footing?

Strangely, though snipers could have opened fire upon us at any moment, I felt no real fear. I had experienced a much greater terror when Frank and Elijah and I had fled through the woods of Mississippi. Now I would soon be able to stand and fight, not flee.

■ ■ ■

As we began to climb, inching our way upwards, the guides instructed us to lock hands to keep from slipping. They led the men up ahead, maneuvering up the steep incline like mountain goats, restrained only by the slowest man in our line. We had to trust their judgment completely. Without their instructions we didn't even know where to place our next footstep.

Directly in front of me was Gunal and behind me was Kurt. Spread out from us were several other lines of climbing men. I heard Gunal wheezing, trying to catch his breath. As we climbed, his breathing became increasingly labored. Would we ever get to the top? I hoped we would not still be climbing at daybreak. Then, without the cover of darkness, we would be sitting ducks for snipers and enemy planes. I forced myself to think of other things. Would Alonzo have been assigned to a fighting unit yet? I wondered if Walter Garland and Ed White would be with him. The Englishman, Gunal, coughed and gasped for breath.

At one point he slipped. Rocks broke loose and sailed past my legs, then took an eternity before crashing into the blackness below. Our line came to a standstill as Gunal struggled to regain his footing. For a moment I thought the entire line would go tumbling downward. We clawed at the rocky earth, moving upwards once more. This must end soon, I thought, it must. We were all beginning to weaken. We had been cautioned not to drink water, and now scalding thirst burned my throat. At that moment I would have given anything for a drink of water.

I could no longer think. I put one foot ahead of the other numbly, following behind Gunal. The climb had become steeper and more treacherous. Minutes seemed like hours. Just when I thought I couldn't take another step, the path evened out. We continued along a plateau toward a bed of rocks where a stream of water spouted out of the ground. Men rushed pell-mell to get to the stream. The guides yelled out, cautioning us not to drink.

We were just to rinse our mouths. There was still a long climb ahead. One comrade disobeyed instructions, and within a moment was writhing on the ground and grasping his stomach against painful cramps. He felt no better as we prepared to continue the climb. The cramps became so intense that he could not get up. The guides shook their heads and signaled for us to move on.

"But what about him?" I asked.

"Nothing can be done," was the answer.

A blanket was thrown over the man and we left him. Hopefully, he would be able to join the next group of men to cross over. I followed our guide in a state of shock. Most of the men were stunned. It was our first taste of what war was all about—death.

Within minutes after beginning the second lap of the climb, we tossed away most of our possessions. Men threw away their knapsacks, coats and blankets; anything to lighten the load. They even took off their socks and flung them into the darkness. I kept my shoes but threw most everything else away. When it came to my books—three battered paperbacks by Claude McKay, Gorky, and Langston Hughes—I paused. I tried to fit them into my pockets but they felt like pieces of lead. I fingered them regretfully, then pulled two out, letting them drop. They flittered down through the blackness. It was like a part of me falling. Later I found the book I still had was the one by Langston Hughes.

Once again in a grueling climb, I felt even worse now after having experienced a brief rest. My fingertips felt raw from grasping the rocks and the limbs of scrubby trees.

I summoned all my will to keep from faltering and reminded myself that everything I wanted was on the other side of the mountains; not only the chance to fight back for once in my life, but a path that might return me with honor to my children.

Top: Oliver Law with unidentified soldier.

Bottom: Braden, Graeber, Taney, Madison, Abramson, McDaniels, Gerber, Chilingarian, unidentified.

Thomas Page

Milton Herndon

Larry Dukes

Claude Pringle

Salaria Kee

Vaughan Love

Crawford Morgan

Abe Lewis

Left: unidentified volunteer.

Below:
Back row: Yliokala
and Jim Ewen from
Canada, Hanson.
Front row: Ted Gibbs from
Chicago, Pete Smith from
NYC, Abramson from
Canada, unidentified.

Right: Alonzo Watson

Below: Dolores Ibarruri (La Pasionaria), first woman ever in Spanish Cabinet.

Top: Leroy Collins (top right) with group of Lincolns returning from Spain.

Right: Pat Roosevelt.

Below: Frank Feingersh, Bill Bois, James Yates, Joe Drill returning home from from Spain.

James Yates and Lorraine Hansberry of Greenwich Village-Chelsea Branch NAACP, protesting the murder of Medger Evers. June 1963.

James Yates marching with Abraham Lincoln Brigade in peace demonstration. NYC June 1982.

James Yates visits memorial in Gandesa, Spain, built after Franco's death to honor those who died for the Republic of Spain.

Chapter 7

Spain

At about five in the morning we arrived at our first Spanish outpost, a monastery. It was midway down the mountain and served as a way station for those who had been forced to take this route into Spain. No monks were there. A few Spanish Loyalists guarded the post, receiving and dispatching volunteers. It struck me that this monastery was much like the places used by the abolitionists who temporarily housed slaves escaping from the plantations of the South in America. We trudged into the bare stone room and flopped down on the floor. A huge fire crackled in the fireplace and we drew close to it for warmth. Those who still had shoes on pulled them off. Many men curled up on the floor and dropped off into a deep sleep, too exhausted to eat the food our Spanish comrades had prepared for us.

"Vamos, amigos!" The guides woke us. It seemed like I had just closed my eyes. We staggered to our feet. The rest period had lasted barely two hours.

Daybreak threw a greyish curtain over the mountains and the valleys. Outside I gazed downwards and saw a fleet of trucks, crawling like ants around the mountain. Could they be coming to the monastery. Who were they?

Maybe fascists, I thought. Perhaps the fascist army had broken through and not only taken Madrid but were now coming to attack us here. We were still unarmed, with no means to defend ourselves, and too weary to reclimb the mountain. The guides, too, were looking at the convoy. They showed no panic. We soon understood that the convoy was our own trucks coming to transport us. As they approached the drivers shouted greetings and we saluted them.

We boarded the trucks and headed down the narrow donkey trail which had been built more for carts than for wide trucks. Mile long drops, without guardrails, loomed around each curve. The drivers enjoyed speeding and laughed good-naturedly at our fear. We were being driven to a fort in Figueras where we would receive our first military training. We had no guns. They were so badly needed at the front that we had to practice with sticks.

For a few days we were housed at the military barracks at Castillo de San Fernando in Figueras, one of the largest fortresses in Spain. During a lull after training we had an opportunity to visit the town of Figueras. It was a small sleepy Mediterranean town. The houses were situated on hilly streets and made of white stucco. The people were friendly, but we sadly learned later that there were many reactionaries among them. Men like myself did not speak a word of Spanish. To order a glass of milk, we would moo like a cow. We cackled like chickens to order eggs, and we touched our bodies to indicate we wanted to use the toilet. This was the way things were during our first few days in Spain.

Ten days after I arrived at the ancient Catalan fortress, I was on a train headed for Albacete, headquarters of the International Brigade of Volunteers. My training to be a soldier had consisted of learning to shoulder and point tree sticks. I had hopes that in Albacete I would get additional training, this time with real guns. I thought of my father's old shotgun. Even it would have been welcome here.

As the train sped through the countryside I recalled conversations I had heard over the past few days. America, Britain and France still refused to aid our side, while Hitler, Mussolini and the fascists in Portugal had stepped up their aid to Franco. In fact, Mussolini's troops had already captured a large area in southern Spain. Mussolini, supported by Hitler's Condor Legion, was most responsible for the gigantic attempt to isolate and capture Madrid.

Heavily outnumbered and outgunned, the Republicans were barely able to withstand the onslaught. The death toll was staggering. How long could the Republicans maintain their resistance against the combined forces of international fascism? It both angered and depressed me that my side, always my side, should forever find itself without proper means to defend its interests. I hoped that President Roosevelt would drop the embargo and aid the Loyalists.

I looked out upon the peaceful countryside. From here the front, with strange names like Jarama and Guadalajara, where the enemy outnumbered us seven to one, seemed far away. I heard no guns and saw no enemy planes. Yellow orange groves and green olive trees stretched to the horizon. Donkey trains wound lazily through the fields and toward the mountains. With the exception of an occasional bombed and shattered building in a few of the towns we passed through, there was no physical evidence that the country was under siege and that at this very moment men were dying at the front.

In the fields peasants went about their harvesting as they had done for thousands of years. Darken their faces and they could have been picking cotton and pulling corn in Mississippi.

As we stopped in the small towns, women and children came up to the train. They were poor, but at each stop they brought baskets of oranges. They gave the usual salute and shouted, *"No pasaran!"* the famous battle cry of the Republicans.

As we traveled southward rumors began to circulate on the train that the fascists had launched another massive attack, that Madrid had fallen, that the Abraham Lincoln Brigade had been annihilated, that the fascists were marching to Albacete and might be there by the time we got there. Then there were counter-rumors that Madrid had not fallen, that the International Brigade and Spanish People's Army were standing firm at Jarama and that the embargo had been lifted!

I seized upon this last rumor. I felt good that my country was on the same side I was fighting on! My comrades had been singing and I joined them, humming tunes I did not know. Somebody came from another coach with a guitar. Everyone on the train was singing. At that moment nobody believed the fascists were in Albacete or that Madrid would ever fall.

We were anxious to get to Albacete. It was situated some ninety miles southwest of Valencia, the provisional capital of Republican Spain, and approximately one hundred miles southeast of Madrid. Before the Civil War it had been a town of forty thousand people, a railway hub for the seaport complex of Cartagena, Alicante and Valencia. It was also the center for the warehousing and shipping of wheat to the surrounding areas. Because of the war the population had more than doubled.

We arrived that afternoon. Just outside of town we had been slowed down by a stream of refugees entering the city. They sat astride emaciated donkeys pulling carts containing their meager belongings. They didn't look up when the train whistled to clear the tracks. They were numbed by a war that forced them to flee their homes.

One of the Spaniards in charge explained that at the outbreak of the Civil War the fascists controlled Albacete. The trade union people and the peasants from the surrounding areas had driven them out after fierce fighting. As the fascists retreated, they brutally executed everyone not in sympathy with them.

We finally pulled into the station and voices singing "The Internationale" greeted us. Every nationality in the world seemed to be represented in the delegation pressing toward the train. We joined in the singing as did a few of the refugees that had found their way to the station. I felt an overwhelming sense of kinship with all the people around me. As a song finished, we applauded vigorously and shouted *"No pasaran!"* Lovely girls gave us flowers.

As I mingled with the delegation of Americans and Spaniards I glimpsed a familiar face. I had stood in bread-lines with him in Chicago and New York, and had attended demonstrations to free the Scottsboro boys and Angelo Herndon. I spotted Walter Garland and he saw me at the same moment. We rushed forth and embraced, then we stood back to look at one another. In New York he had worn a perpetual frown as if he were absorbed with some deep inner confusion. He seldom cracked a smile. But now his chocolate face and almost slanted brown eyes beamed at me. Under his pencil-thin moustache his full lips broke into a generous smile, which gave him a peaceful inner glow. He didn't seem like the tense and taciturn Walter Garland I had known before. He was like a new man.

Walter Garland lived in Brooklyn, New York, before going to Spain. He quit school at an early age to help support his family. His mother died almost before he could remember, leaving him with his father and five sisters. I remember Walter when he was active in the Brooklyn Negro National Congress. He always said the most important discovery of his youth was the realization that what was happening locally to oppressed people was happening the world over.

"I saw Admiral Kilpatrick this morning," Garland said, grinning. "He arrived yesterday. He said you and he and Vaughan Love were on the same boat and that you'd be coming. How was the climb?"

"Rough."

We made our way out from the station. Everyone was singing as they marched down the street. A blur of faces continued to come up and shake my hand and to congratulate Walter Garland. I noticed he walked with a limp. I soon discovered that he had been wounded in the Battle of Jarama, shot in the groin. He had also been promoted to lieutenant. He now awaited a new assignment. I kept glancing at him. This was somebody who had actually fought at the front!

Despite the limp there was confidence in his stride. His shoulders were thrown back. The smile upon his lips remained easy as we shook hands with well-wishers. He wore his wound like a badge of honor, almost as if it had been an initiation into manhood.

I felt a twinge of envy. Though it became clear that nearly half of the men in the Lincoln Brigade with whom Walter had fought had lost their lives in the defense of Madrid, I felt no less eager to get to the front. It seemed as if more than ever, the quality of my own life for the rest of my days depended on it.

"On the train we heard that Madrid had fallen," I told him.

"Franco's propaganda," he replied. "Every day he releases a statement to the press that we've been defeated. The reactionaries print the rubbish, hoping it is true."

"I also heard that President Roosevelt had taken America out of the embargo," I said hopefully.

"Wishful thinking," Walter replied grimly. "Roosevelt is only one man. Look at the composition of Congress, the Senate, the Ku Klux Klan mentality throughout our government. You think they're going to allow Roosevelt to side with us? It will never happen. They'd be much more comfortable with a Nazi and fascist victory."

People cheered us from the sidewalks. Donkeys and carts thronged the street about us, many still carrying refugees while the others carried war supplies. Walter said that Douglas Roach and Sterling Rochester had also been in the battle to save Madrid, and that Oliver Law, who had been so helpful to me in Chicago, so distinguished himself on the battlefield that he had been promoted to head a machine gun company. He didn't say a word about Alonzo and yet for some reason I found myself hesitating to ask about my friend.

We left the main road and were on our way to the quarters where my group would be housed, when I said, "and Alonzo?"

For the first time the old frown came back into Walter's face. "They caught Alonzo," he said quietly. "They caught Alonzo in the neck."

"He's in the hospital?" I asked.

"No. He's dead."

I wasn't sure I heard him right. "Dead?" It wasn't possible. I was shocked at the news. Within me it seemed as if the world was standing still. My best friend, Alonzo, dead.

My mind went back to the loft in the Village where we had spent so many happy days together. I remembered our many trips to Harlem. I remembered the nights we attended the meetings against war and fascism, and those hours in Union Square, listening and getting educated about world events. I was once again at the dock the night he left for Spain, telling myself we were only temporarily separated, that we would be together again. We would fight together. But now Alonzo was dead.

I was angry, more angry than I had ever been before in my life. I stood up and shouted, "Damn fascists. Damn the fascists. Damn Franco, Hitler, and damn that Mussolini!" Only months ago Mussolini's troops raped and ran over Ethiopia. Back home there was the Ku Klux Klan and the Bilbos. I decided at that moment that being angry was not enough. I pledged to be a part of the people's struggle in Spain, at home, wherever in the world people were fighting for freedom. Then I realized Walter was speaking to me.

"He died at the battle of Jarama. The International Brigades included the Irish, French, Blacks, and many others. Alonzo was with the Lincoln Battalion. Frank Ryan was with the James Connolly Column. It's named after a martyred leader of the Irish Easter Rebellion back in 1916. Ryan is here. He may be able to tell more about Alonzo."

I remembered back home in Mississippi reading about the Irish rebellion and wondering even then whether we Blacks would also revolt against the system in the South.

"When can I see him?" I asked.

"I'll bring him with me tomorrow."

The next morning I met with Ryan, along with Walter and a couple of other men who were with the Lincoln Brigade. Ryan began to speak first about his company. Although I wanted to hear about Alonzo, I forced myself to be patient and to listen.

He explained that the Irish volunteers were among the first internationals to have arrived in Spain. They reflected the spirit of some of their great leaders, freedom fighters like Terence MacSwiney, Maude Gonne, and James Larkin. On the Aragon front they fought with the German Thaelmann Brigade. Besides himself, there was a Catholic minister named John McGrotty and John Joseph O'Reilly who fought in the "Miracle of October," when the fascists were repelled from Madrid. Slowly he began to talk about how the International Brigades dug in at Jamara. There had been men of the Lincoln Battalion, Thaelmanns, French, British, Franco-Belgian as well as regular Spanish troops.

"On the road from Chinchon to Madrid, that same road we marched to the attack just three days earlier," Captain Ryan continued, "we were now badly scattered. All of us who had survived, a few hundred Britons, Irish and Spaniards, were dispirited by the heavy casualties, by the defeat, and by lack of food. We were exhausted after three days of heavy fighting. Our men appeared to have reached the end of their resistance. Some were still straggling down the slopes, returning from what had been the front line just hours earlier. Now there was no line. There was nothing between the Madrid Road and the fascists but disorganized groups of weary, war-wrecked men. Groups of hungry men lay about on the roadside, eating oranges that had been flung to them by a passing lorry. This was not the time to sort them into units.

"I noticed with satisfaction that some men brought spare rifles back with them from the battle. My eyes kept straying up and down the hill we just vacated. I hitched a rifle to my shoulder. The others around me recognized this was a signal to return to battle and they stumbled to their feet. We headed back up the hill. 'Fall in behind us' was yelled back and forth, and 'Hurry up.' Back we marched, nearer and nearer the front. Stragglers still in retreat down the slopes halted in amazement, changed direction and ran to join us. Men lying exhausted on the road jumped up, cheered and joined the ranks. I looked back. What a strange band. Unshaven, unkempt, blood-stained, and grimy, but full of fight again and marching on the road back. We passed the Spanish Battalion. They too got the infection and began singing as they deployed to the right. The French and the Franco-Belgian troops joined us.

"Straight ahead of us were little cones of blue-red flame, which let us know where the Moorish and German machine gunners were. Oh, for just a few grenades! We called to one another to coordinate our fire on those cones. We pushed forward inch by inch while darkness fell. As we advanced, they began to retreat. In actual disappointment we shouted, 'The bastards won't wait for our bayonets!' Madrid was saved, but the dead and the wounded were many."

"How did Alonzo die?" I finally asked. Captain Ryan did not reply. One of the Blacks, Doug Roach, told the story:

"Deep trenches extended along each side of the road. Sandbags had been placed across the road to protect us. One was exposed from the knees up while crossing. During February 25th and 26th the Lincoln Brigade suffered twelve casualties there. Alonzo Watson was one."

I thought of those dates and realized at that very time I was steaming across the ocean, not realizing I would never see my friend Alonzo again.

■ ■ ■

While Madrid was surrounded by fascist forces, Hitler's hand-picked leader, Heinz Trettner, headed Fighter Squadron 88 which bombed the city mercilessly, day and night. Later in the spring of 1937 Trettner would be responsible for the bombing of the peaceful Basque country towns of Durango and Guernica (March 31 and April 26, respectively). Picasso portrayed the brutal bombing in his world-renowned painting *Guernica*. The systematic bombings of civilian populations were, to the German generals, experiments in demoralizing the enemy's resistance and experiments in designing the blitzkrieg offense. The results of these experiments were used when Germany invaded Poland in September, 1939.

Later in the war I, too, would be in the fight to save Madrid, at Brunete. As a truck driver I would experience the war from a broader perspective; sometimes deep in the rear, in cities and villages where people sweated and toiled to support men at the front. As we drove the highways we often passed women, children and older men braving the fascist airplanes as they harvested the fields.

Among the men in transport there were many ambulance drivers. Day after day I witnessed men who went without sleep for days. These men were so committed to saving the wounded that they risked their own lives.

Very often during lulls we would have a chance to rest. To my surprise, when we arrived in Spain, we had a payday. We would receive something like thirty pesetas every week, the same pay as the Spanish army regulars. Often, when we were near a small town or village, we would donate some of our money toward a feast for the children. One peseta would buy a drink, and five would pay for a good meal. Our contributions for the children went a long way.

Getting together, we would exchange our many different experiences. I listened to the various tongues and accents. When hearing the Irish brogue, my thoughts would return to Mississippi, back when I was a boy. I recalled Mr. Gus, who gave my Uncle Willie ammunition and told him to defend himself from the lynchers.

The first few days in Albacete were a deeply emotional time for me, especially after I learned that my best friend Alonzo was gone. Added to this misery was the old army barracks where I spent nights. It was built around the sixteenth century to house no more than three hundred soldiers. There were now two thousand volunteers housed within. The sanitary conditions were unbelievable. Men were compelled to use the open yards for a toilet. I never slept a wink throughout the long night. The only thing of comfort was knowing what my assignment was. I was scheduled to leave in the morning for the Auto-Park.

The Auto-Park in Albacete was one of many services that aided the fighting at the front. Our job was to see that the trucks and cars kept rolling. Only a few men were skilled mechanics out of an international work force of about one hundred. The others would become truck drivers after having learned enough to make minor repairs when breakdowns occurred on the road. Imagine my surprise when I was told that the Admiral had been assigned to the Auto-Park as a truck driver!

Albacete by early spring of 1937 had become a United Nations of a special kind. Men and women of all different tongues and nationalities, young and old, all came together to fight side by side with the Spanish people. The Spaniards were not only fighting to save themselves and their country from fascism but Europe and the whole world from plunging into the horror of war.

As the days passed I found out the Auto-Park was not immune from war casualties. Once an enemy truck was captured on the southern front, near the city of Almeria. It was hauled into the Park for repairs. One of our German comrades discovered a hand grenade among the rubbish left in the truck. He attempted to take it outside of the Park to safety but it exploded in his hand. He lost his right arm.

More than once, in the quiet of the night, I was awakened by a burst of rifle fire. Albacete, like many other parts of Republican Spain, had its saboteurs behind the front lines.

As the war intensified the need for more well-trained mechanics became critical. I learned from a new arrival that a young Black would arrive soon from Detroit, Michigan. His name was Kanute Oliver Frankson, and he worked for the Ford Motor Company as a chief mechanic. He had played a leading role in organizing the union there. Frankson would become the Chief Mechanic for the International Transport.

One day in April my head was under the hood of a Russian truck which I was attempting to repair when I heard a familiar voice ring out, "Jimmy! Man, I knew I'd find you here in Spain!"

I was so surprised that I bumped my head against the hood in my haste to see if it was really Joe Taylor. I grabbed him and shook his hand vigorously. I forgot my greasy hands until I saw the big spot that I left on his white shirt. But what was a little grease between two good friends who had found each other in faraway Spain?

I knew Joe from Harlem. He was just as committed as I was to the struggles of the thirties, specifically as the movement occurred in Harlem. In a matter of minutes I must have asked him a hundred questions about what was happening back home. He told me that more and more of the American people had become aware of the menace of fascism. This news was gratifying indeed. We stood leaning against the truck talking about things we had been through together and of people we knew.

I was so caught up in the conversation with Joe that I forgot that the truck had to be ready to leave for the front by noon. I just had to cut our conversation short and say good-bye. We were at war and that took precedence over everything else.

I gave him my elbow this time, not wanting to chance making more of a mess. He laughed and took it. Then we both sobered, perhaps realizing at the same time that we would probably never see one another again. He nodded a little, then turned and started walking along the narrow unpaved street, never looking back. I stood there watching until he disappeared from sight.

Eight months later, from my hospital bed in Orihuela, I was told that Joe Taylor had made quite a name for himself by his courageous fighting at Brunete. He was pinned deep behind enemy lines on the Aragon front near the town of Fuentes. He spent the greater part of a day within three yards of burnt out Republican tanks before somehow making it back to our lines.

Later, during July, after crossing the Ebro, Joe took part in the fighting at Gandesa. In that battle the first, second and third companies all lost their commissars. Two Blacks were shot. Tom Page, a sergeant of the third company, and Joe Taylor of the first company. Joe took a bullet through the shoulder. A report that I read stated that, "Sergeant Joe Taylor, of the first company, was a very courageous veteran of every action since, and including, Brunete."

Sunday was a day of rest at the Auto-Park. Even the mess hall closed after the morning coffee. The one pleasant thing about a day off was that there were always new arrivals with news from home. Two other things to look forward to were the bullfight and the late meal out, nine o'clock in the evening, a rather late time to be dining for most of us. I can still see the line-up in front of the town's biggest hotel with everyone's tongues hanging out.

On Sunday the Admiral and I went to a bullfight together. I had read Ernest Hemingway's version of bull-fighting, but what we saw wasn't quite like the way he described it. To be truthful, I'll never understand the real art of this sport that brings huge crowds to their feet. At the time I could only see blood and danger. From behind where we were sitting I heard a rather familiar yell during the kill. Looking back, I saw James Roberson and Oliver Law. I wondered if Law had been exposed to bullfighting on the ranch in his native state, Texas.

Oliver Law, James Roberson and I had all been together in the youth movement on the Chicago South Side. We were all in the march to Springfield, demanding home relief and social security for the unemployed workers. Knowing that Roberson had organized and led many protest demonstrations against Mussolini's invasion of Ethiopia, it didn't surprise me at all to meet him again in Spain. Jim, as we called him, was now a cook in the Lincoln Brigade. Men who were with him said that whenever there was a shortage or he ran out of rations, Jim would turn to the land for food. They said he made the best olive pies in all of Spain.

■ ■ ■

It wasn't unusual for a train of internationals to arrive in Albacete on Sunday, but this Sunday we expected a train filled with young men from France, England, and other European countries as far away as Finland. Also among this group were suppose to be some seventy-five Americans, Black and white.

Early in the morning we got the news that these men would be arriving some time around midday. Among so many Americans we were sure there would be some of our friends from back home. This hot, sunny day in June, the train arrived a few minutes late. It was easy to spot Blacks as they unloaded from the train. The first one I spotted was Charles Youngblood, a seaman from Harlem. Walking next to him was Milton Herndon, the brother of Angelo Herndon. By this time, the Admiral began to yell, "Walter! Here's Walter Cobbs!" and gave an even louder yell when he spotted Leroy Collins of Cleveland, Ohio.

When the excitement died down and the introductions were over, I asked the Admiral why there were so many Black volunteers from Ohio. He began to explain by drawing a map of Ohio. "The fight against slavery began early in Ohio, it was the major route of the Underground Railway, an escape route for slaves en route to Canada. Despite the work of abolitionists like Harriet Tubman and Sojourner Truth, Ohio was one of the most racially bigoted states north of the Mason-Dixon line. Even today Blacks are barred from certain hotels and restaurants, and the movie houses are segregated. Black unemployment and poverty are chronic."

Through learning these facts I came to understand why so many brave young Black men and women from Ohio went to Spain: Walter Cobb, Claude Pringle, Bernard Rucker, Edward Johnson, Leroy Collins, Salaria Kee, Abraham Lewis, Walter Dicks, Admiral Kilpatrick.

Later in the war I got to know more about Walter Cobb. I remember him telling us of a big scare he had behind the lines of the Aragon Front, where he was the only American with the French Brigade. He spoke both French and Spanish.

"I have to keep in practice with my languages in this country, man," he said and went on, "If I didn't know Spanish during this last battle I'd have been taken for a Moor and made a prisoner. Man, I was driving a captured truck that we took at Beichite one night, driving it back behind our lines to be repaired. I didn't have time to paint over the Falangist markings on the truck. I hadn't gone but a few kilometers in the dark before some Loyalist soldiers on patrol duty, Spanish boys, stopped me at a crossroad and beamed their flashlights on the truck. When they saw the fascist insignia, and then saw how dark I was, they thought for sure I was a Moor that got lost and came across the lines by accident. They yelled at me to jump down with my hands up and they held their cocked guns at my head. Man, I started talking Spanish right away, explaining I was with the Internationals. They let me show them my papers and I told them how we captured that truck from the fascists and that it belonged to us now. Then they almost hugged me! But suppose I didn't know enough Spanish? Looking like a Moor as I do, I might have been shot by my own side! It pays to habla espanol."

■ ■ ■

The nature of my work at the Auto-Park allowed me to meet all kinds of people. I was in contact with ambulance drivers, nurses and doctors. I soon discovered the horrific conditions the medical people endured.

I was on the greeting committee for Dr. Arnold Donawa, a well known dental surgeon from Harlem and a graduate of Howard University. He was one of over a hundred doctors, nurses and ambulance drivers from the American Medical Bureau.

Dr. Donawa left Albacete for a grueling period of work at the front. After that he was given charge of the jaw surgery department at Vallacre.

Later Dr. Donawa was to talk about some of the conditions in Spain during the war.

"We suffered above all from a lack of instruments and supplies needed for adequate surgery. Frequently we didn't have enough gauze and bandages to dress the wounds of men. There was such a great scarcity of the elementary medical supplies that we had to unwind the bandage one man had used, have it washed and boiled, and then rewind it and use it again on another patient.

Sometimes it was hard to get the old bloodstains entirely out, but we managed to sterilize the old bandages and made them fit for use."

"We did not have a drop of novocaine in the hospital and I thought I might be able to get some with the move. And I did, but not enough, only a thousand ampules. This as well as many other indispensable drugs were almost unobtainable in Spain in those final days. There were so many items; things we take for granted back home we lacked in Spain. To reduce jaw fractures, for example, we needed a special kind of very thin stainless steel wire. If I had had just a pound of it we could have relieved the crisis at the hospital for months. But we didn't have it, nor did we have any X-ray film. We had to work by touch to determine the number of fractures."

After the war Dr. Donawa returned to his dental practice in Harlem and generously donated his services to the returning veterans of Spain.

Among the Black volunteers to the medical team was Salaria Kee, the only Black nurse to serve in the International Brigades. When we met in Spain I recalled having met her earlier in New York. That was shortly after she had arrived there from Ohio and Alonzo and I were very active in Harlem protesting Mussolini's invasion of Ethiopia.

In Spain I saw Salaria just before she was called to Teruel, a town on the front lines. The story has it that the news spread among the men in the deep trenches near Teruel that a Black nurse was about to arrive. A Spanish coin was flipped to decide who was going to meet her, and Oliver Law won. However, this posed a problem as Law was too big to fit into the only half-decent uniform they could come up with. Thus, the honor of greeting Salaria fell to Douglas Roach, a smaller man, one of the first Blacks to come to Spain.

Chapter 8
_____

Brunete

I couldn't quite believe what I was hearing when on
June 28, 1937, I was told "You will be leaving for the front."
I went back to the barracks to pick up a few belongings
and to say good-bye to the English cook. Then I rushed
over to the Auto-Park to say a special good-bye to
Kilpatrick and to my German friend Gaffner.

The old Russian truck which I would be driving
waited for me. It had been filled to the brim with war supplies, so I assumed that I had been assigned to the Lincoln
Brigade. A young German soldier who spoke only broken
English was in the truck. I had trouble understanding what
he was saying but shortly it dawned on me that I had been
assigned to the German International Brigade called the
Thaelmann.

That I would not be with the Lincoln Brigade was
totally unexpected. I knew the Thaelmann Brigade was
made up of anti-fascist Germans, just as the MacKenzie-
Papineau Brigade was composed of Canadians and the
Garibaldi group of Italians, and other groups for the
French, Belgian, Irish and English. As an American,
shouldn't I have been assigned to the Lincoln Brigade?
Here I was with a young German lieutenant, with whom I
could barely communicate, on my way to join a Brigade

whose language I didn't understand. How would I ever convince them to allow me to fight when we reached the front?

The lieutenant made several attempts at conversation. The old Russian truck creaked and groaned as we drove throughout the night. The war had taken its toll on the lieutenant, who looked as though he had been pushed to the limit.

I drove down the road thinking that I should not blame him for my assignment. He was just doing his duty, and I had to do mine. I made an extra effort to communicate with him, as he bravely struggled with his English. I was amazed that we began to understand one another. He told me that he fought at Guadalajara and Madrid. He lifted one of his hands and I saw that four of his fingers were twisted and broken. He opened his shirt and I noticed a mound of burnt flesh near his heart. Before coming to Spain he had been a student at Heidelberg University. His family were socialists. One sister had fled to the United States, but the rest of his family members were in a concentration camp somewhere west of Berlin. The only way he could resist Hitler was by fighting against fascism in Spain. He showed me a picture that startled me. It was a picture of him standing in the front of a line of soldiers shaking hands with a large Black man sporting a broad smile. I recognized the man whose autograph was at the bottom of the picture: Paul Robeson.

A warmth stirred within me when I saw that picture. I knew that Robeson was in Spain, singing to the Republican forces near the front. I tried to explain in Spanish to the lieutenant how I thought there was no other man or woman who represented freedom for mankind more than did Paul Robeson, and about his endless struggle for the rights of the Black people. Occasionally I would say "Comprende?" and he would reply "Si, si."

But eventually the lieutenant got sleepy. Discreetly he would wet his eyelids with saliva to keep them open. He knew the roads and nodded his head from time to time to keep me going in the right direction.

While I drove I thought of the other talented and famous people that were supporting us. By reading the two newspapers, *Wall* and *Our Fight,* which were available at Albacete, I learned that support was growing all over the world. Among the supporters were some prominent Black citizens—T. Arnold Hill of the National Urban League, who later became the highest appointed Black in the Roosevelt administration, Reverend William Lloyd Imes, one of Harlem's great churchmen, Ferdinand Smith, a vice-president of the National Maritime Union, and Richard Wright, author of *Blackboy* and *Native Son.*

Hollywood and Broadway stars gave of their time and talent by collecting thousands of dollars to purchase sorely needed medical supplies. Ninety-eight American writers, including Brooks Atkinson, Erskine Caldwell, John Dewey, Sinclair Lewis, Thornton Wilder, Christopher Morley, Robert Benchley, Clifton Fadiman, Dorothy Parker and Dorothy Canfield Fisher signed a communique condemning Franco and the US embargo.

The lieutenant tried to stay awake. He rolled around in his seat and asked, "And America, is it true they hang Blacks from trees there?"

For some reason this question embarrassed me, but I had to reply, "Yes."

I could have told him about the National Guardsman in Springfield who tried to kick my eye out, or of the detective on the freight train who stomped on my hand, but I didn't. I could have explained that my family was in a kind of concentration camp, too, although they were not restrained by barbed wire. Our wire was invisible except where it manifested itself in signs like "White Only," and where it erupted into a lynching. I could have said that, but I didn't.

When we arrived just outside of the ruins of Guadalajara, we were greeted by about a thousand Thaelmanns who had been waiting for us. The movement of the brigade had been held up by a lack of supplies. Eager soldiers pounced on the ammunition and loaded their rifles and machine guns. A few of the fortunate soldiers got themselves some hand grenades. Some even got gas masks before the supply ran out.

Most of the men were momentarily surprised to see a Black driver. When the lieutenant introduced me to the Germans, They bowed in their formal way, then shook hands letting me know they were very grateful that I was there. I soon learned that three of their previous drivers had been killed, two at Jarama.

The soldiers fell into formation and began marching. I joined the line behind two other trucks containing food and water. A song rose softly from the ranks into the air. They sang in German and I vaguely recognized the tune of "Freiheit." There was a kind of strange beauty about the singing and the marching under the bright light of the moon. The fascists were somewhere in the distance. This could be the last march many of the men would ever make.

Just before daylight the marching Thaelmanns took cover in dense woods outside El Escorial, a small town northwest of Madrid. Its world-famous royal residence, also the burial place for the Spanish monarchs, would become staff headquarters. I learned later that it was the safest place in Spain. It would be spared by the rebel air force which wished to avoid waking the dead Spanish royal families—generations of kings and queens dating back to the Middle Ages.

No one knew the hour or day the Thaelmann Brigade would be entering into the battle. On July 4, 1937, I made my first trip to the front. I needed to familiarize myself with the roads and the area. My companion on that first day at the front was a young German lad who looked no more than seventeen years old. He had already faced the fascists at other fronts. Our first stop, the little town of Brunete, had been totally destroyed by bombs. Only one building, a barn, remained standing. The only life in the whole village was a few stray cats and hungry dogs. The people had all been killed by the bombs dropped by the fascist planes, or, perhaps some had escaped. My German friend and I were the only two people in the whole town. Still, only minutes after we arrived, wave after wave of Heinkel II's swept the skies. I ran under a culvert for cover, while my young friend just stood staring up at the sky. To calm me down he finally crawled into the culvert with me. Bombs began to fall, completely drowning out the sound of rifle fire just beyond the hill.

My first job was to take food from where it was prepared in El Escorial to the troops on the front lines. Alone, I started out with my truck loaded with large containers of thick bean soup, round loaves of bread, and as much water as space would allow. I was unarmed, as all of the guns were needed on the front line. Smoke filled the air, making visibility impossible. The road which was filled with deep craters made by artillery shells, was clogged with trucks, ambulances and donkey carts.

I arrived in Brunete about eleven in the morning. In an open field next to that one remaining barn was an ambulance. The driver stood a few feet away from it. I felt sure he would be able to tell me where to find the Thaelmanns. Before I could reach him two swift fighter planes swooped down from the sky and raked the field with machine gunfire. I then heard the sound of bombers approaching and began to make a dash to the barn. Up until that time I hadn't noticed the tall red-headed lad who yelled, "Don't go into that building!" At the same time he waved in the direction of a foxhole near the road. I don't even know his name, but he saved my life. Before I reached the foxhole, the barn took a direct hit and was nothing but a massive blaze of fire.

Small planes continued diving so low that I could see the pilots' faces. When I reached the foxhole I found three men already wedged into the space barely big enough for two. I climbed in on top of them pulling a branch over us. I could hear bullets hitting as they grazed close enough to knock leaves from the branch. One of the men jumped out of the foxhole and started shouting in perfect English, "Bastards. Fascist bastards!" He turned out to be an Englishman from Liverpool. When I asked about the location of the Thaelmanns, he said he knew where they were and would show me the way. Driving in my truck, we turned off the main road onto a dry parched field where tanks and trucks had created a path. As we approached a ridge, the path veered into a gully just a few yards away from a wooded area. Here the path ended. I could see a few soldiers from the Thaelmann Brigade leading donkeys with large empty baskets on their backs. Under a big tree lay several dead and wounded soldiers. We quickly unloaded the food from the truck. Some of the soldiers placed it in the donkey baskets. Then the donkey train moved slowly into the deep-dug trench that led to the left side of the ridge, where the Thaelmann Brigade joined the battle at Brunete. I knew from the rifle fire that fierce fighting was taking place. The sky was full of planes.

As I returned to El Escorial I saw that nothing remained along the roadside. German Henkel IIIs and Junker 52s were dropping bombs on the road. I stopped the truck beside a steep ridge and scaled it so as to be able to see the dogfight which was taking place between the fascist planes and our Soviet-built Mosca fighter planes. I yelled out, "Get him, knock them bastards out of the sky!" In the meantime I was being bothered by bugs and tried to brush them away. One of these bugs came so close to my head that I could feel the heat. Suddenly I realized they were not bugs. They were bullets! In less than a second I rolled down the embankment to safety.

When I finally got back to El Escorial I realized that I had been so busy that I had forgotten to eat. I walked to the outpost hospital where I usually ate. There I saw rows and rows of wounded men lying on the floor, in the yard and even in the dining room. I had to step over the wounded to get to the table. Ambulances continued arriving with more wounded. I looked into the faces of the ambulance drivers who had no time to rest, and some looked like death itself. They had been working around the clock and had themselves been under fire many times. They were bringing the wounded from the American Lincoln Brigade, the Franco-Belgian Sixth of February Battalion, the German Thaelmann Brigade, the Canadian MacPaps and, of course, the Spanish, who played the major role in the battle at Brunete.

It was about the twelfth of July when I made an early-morning trip to the front, because I would be driving to Madrid later that day. I often passed the same ambulance driver on my way and we would always wave to one another. This morning he waved me to a stop. From across the road he told me, "Hey, Oliver is dead. They killed Oliver Law."

With me in the open-bodied truck this hot July day were four German comrades, three of them sitting in the back of the truck, and one, dead, lying in a wooden casket draped in black. His remains were to be buried in Madrid. I was very quiet. My thoughts were with Oliver Law. I recalled the first time I heard of him in Chicago, and dwelled on our march to Springfield. He had made history on the battlefields of Spain and now he was dead. He was the first Black man in US history to become the commander of a mostly white unit.

We passed through University City on the outskirts of Madrid. Only a shell of a building remained of what was once the greatest study center in Spain. A mile further along the road we entered the cemetery. I stopped the truck near a pine tree that was needleless from bombs that had been dropped by the fascists. As this German comrade was laid to rest he was surrounded by his own people and a few others from Madrid. I looked across at the hundreds of graves of other Internationals who died in this war.

Oliver Law was buried at the front, below Mosquito Ridge, his grave marked only with a post that had his helmet attached to it. On his helmet they wrote his name and age, thirty-four years old. Steve Nelson, who had assumed command of the Brigade, composed Oliver's eulogy: "Someday, the working class of America will properly acknowledge the role this brave Negro Communist played in the fight for freedom."

The following day I was back at the front. I had unloaded food from my truck into the baskets on the backs of the donkeys. Then, all at once, all hell broke out. The poor animals screamed. I looked up and saw wave after wave of bombers and fighters coming through the sky toward us. There were so many of them that they blotted out the sun. Everybody scattered. Once the road was cleared of donkey carts, I headed toward the scorched field which led to the main road. I spotted a few men scrambling beneath a doorway under a grass mound, jumped out of the truck, and entered behind them. There underground was an area large enough to conceal large artillery guns. A tall man with a black moustache demanded, "Whose bloody truck is that up there?" I knew from his speech that he was an Englishman.

"Sir?"

"That your bloody truck? Well I'm sorry, ol' chap, but you'll simply have to move it. It's drawing fire."

"Sorry."

I climbed outside. Although the whole area was almost as black as night, I'd been given an order. My truck was attracting enemy fire.

The earth bounced under my rubbery legs like the deck of the ship that had brought me across the Atlantic. Each bomb tore open a new hole. Mounds of earth and white-hot shrapnel flew about me. Suddenly I felt a sudden stinging in my legs, but with so much happening I didn't think any more about it. At moments the entire world seemed to be flying upwards, further darkening and polluting the already thick sulfurous air.

The truck still stood where I left it, as though it was immune to destruction. I crawled toward it. My mind felt like it was on fire and my eardrums throbbed with the deafening sounds of exploding bombs. I coughed violently and tried to think less of the planes above, and to force my fingers to do what they were supposed to do. The truck wouldn't start. I could smell the gas as it primed the carburetor. Finally the engine started and I felt relieved. I floored the gas pedal just as an artillery shell hit the rocky earth and exploded behind the truck. The force of the blast sent the truck into the air. As it hit the earth the jolt felt like that of a plane landing and rolling endlessly down the runway. I found myself speeding over the open plain, which only a few days earlier had been a wheatfield surrounded by olive groves.

I finally came to a deep narrow rutted road that had been created by tanks. Completely lost, I stopped the engine and tried to determine from the sound of the shooting just where the battle was taking place. It seemed as though the front line was to my rear. I felt something oozing from my legs, looked down and saw blood. In an attempt to find help, I drove slowly along the gully road. Soon I arrived at a crossroads with a sign that indicated it was twenty kilometers in one direction to Madrid and forty kilometers in the other to El Escorial. I turned toward El Escorial and began to make my way slowly across the barren countryside to the hospital.

When I arrived at the hospital I saw many wounded waiting to see a doctor. I dared not ask for treatment, but bandaged my own legs before crossing the roadway to the Thaelmann Headquarters. There the lieutenant in charge took one look at me, then issued me another assignment for the coming days.

Upon returning to the front, I found the Thaelmann Brigade running low on food. I was assigned to forage the countryside for rations. The Brigade quartermaster, a lieutenant, and I set out in the truck before daylight and I drove along the back roads which took us south of Madrid. After an hour of driving we began to see signs of life—green fields, trees with green leaves, and a flowing river! Along the banks of the river peasant women were washing clothes. Women, children and men were leaving their tiny village for the fields. This was different from what I had known back in Mississippi. Our villages were right in the field with corn and cotton growing at our doorsteps. In Spain the tillers of the earth had, if little else, some traditional communal life after a day in the fields.

By noon we had purchased half a load of food —mostly potatoes, beans and peas. We stopped for a rest in the shade of a large olive tree. From this point which was on a hillside we could see a number of small villages. Each village in Spain, no matter how small, had a steepled church. In the war zones there was nothing peaceful about them, because that is where the snipers hid. We headed towards the largest village we could see to conclude our food purchases. The friendly woman who ran one of the shops where we bought food offered to cook a meal for us, a Spanish tradition. She showed us her garden where she gathered some green peas, scallions, and eggs from the hen house. Before long we were eating a Spanish omelette complete with home-baked bread and wine. It was the best meal I ate during all of my time in Spain. Before we finished our meal the news had spread that a Black man was in town. The whole village came over to see their first Black human being.

It was almost sundown when we got started on our way back to El Escorial, ten kilometers from the battle lines. I took the same narrow roads back to headquarters, avoiding the rebel planes which preyed on the main roads.

I drove a Zig, a Russian-made half-ton truck which proved
to be one of the best trucks for traveling the roads of
Spain. The Zig's only flaw was the tires. They could not
take the Spanish sun and would peel. All too often I would
hear them flap against the macadam.

Back in El Escorial I was told to quickly unload the
truck and to leave at once for Albacete where a load of
supplies was waiting to be picked up. First I would drive to
Madrid where I could sleep for a few hours. Normally the
trip from El Escorial to Madrid took about two hours. But
on this dark night it would take longer. The narrow road
was clogged with all kinds of vehicles, some with dim
headlights and others with no headlights at all. Strung
along the road were donkey carts, with sometimes as many
as three people riding bareback. The traffic moved so slow,
and I was so tired, that I fell asleep at the wheel. I was
awakened when I bumped into the truck ahead of me, but
no damage was done. Eventually I came to a dim glow of
fire on the right side of the road. Coming nearer I realized
that it was University City. Spain's highest institution of
learning was ablaze again.

I reached my destination, a windowless old building
situated in the center of Madrid. This was the domicile of
the Internationals, where I would sleep for the night. I fell
into a deep sleep immediately. While dreaming about
bombs falling on the Brunete front, I was awakened by the
man on watch who was directing everybody to take cover
in the subway. The nearest station was three blocks away.
Madrid was experiencing one of its worst bombardments
and the building was no longer safe. The city was without
lights, but between shells bursting and the glow of falling
bombs, everything could be seen as easily as in light.

I was wide awake by the time we reached the station.
No more dreaming about falling bombs; this was the real
thing! I walked down a flight of dimly lit stairs. There were
so many people on the platform that I decided to walk
along the tracks to the far end of the station. The trains

stopped running at midnight, and it was later than that. A man reached down to help me up from the tracks, and others made a place for me to sit. I looked around the crowded platform and realized that thousands of people spent their nights below ground. It had become a way of life in Madrid.

I looked to my right and sitting against the wall was a man wearing the same kind of driver's uniform as mine. We waved to one another. I tried talking to him but it was impossible for us to hear one another. A kind man exchanged places with me and I moved over to the young man. We exchanged names and I found out he was Barney Rucker, from Columbus, Ohio. The two of us talked on through the night about mutual friends and about the war. Sleeping in that crowded subway amongst the rats was impossible anyway.

The first thing I did when I came out of the subway in the morning was to see if my truck had withstood the bombing. I had no more than climbed into my truck when I heard the drone of a single plane overhead. Suddenly the streets emptied again as people hurried down into the subway stations and disappeared into the basements of buildings. I parked the truck but didn't need to get out and run for cover, as the plane had already passed over. In the distance I could hear it unload bombs, perhaps again upon the University and the districts where working-class people lived.

I was about to depart from Madrid on route back to Albacete. The driving was treacherous with people walking out onto the street. There were so few cars and trucks in Spain that the people were not used to them, so we had to be constantly on guard. I thought, with regret, about the last time I was in Madrid. An old man, without looking or stopping at the curb, walked into the path of my truck. There was no way I could have missed him. Instinctively, I slowed down and was going to assist him, but the lieutenant who rode with me at that time demanded that I keep going.

"It's war time," he barked, "You know damn well that men are dying at the front trying to save Madrid. To save Madrid is to save Spain." We sped on. I have often wondered if the truck killed that elderly man.

Crawford Morgan, a Black volunteer whose background was similar to my own, had a similar story, but he did stop. A few days before Christmas of 1937 a freeze blanketed the Pyrenees. On the Aragon front, all the narrow roads were snow-covered and icy slick. Crawford was determined to deliver food to his comrades in the frozen trenches at the front, where a furious battle was raging. He saw a comrade lying on the road and stopped to investigate. While attempting to pull the soldier off the road, Crawford too was shot and wounded. The saddest fact was that the man Crawford tried to save was already dead.

■ ■ ■

One day my Russian-made truck suffered a serious breakdown. A telephone call to the Auto-Park in Valencia brought a tow truck. When I was towed in I asked how long I would have to wait before the truck was repaired. I was told it would be at least a week, so I volunteered for another assignment. A call came in from a hospital in a little seacoast town, Benicasim. They wanted a driver for a two-day trip to Barcelona. It was only a short trip to Benicasim. It was a clear day with not a spot of cloud in the sky. Most of the wounded, some who were on cots, and others who could be moved around, were all outside bathing in the sun. Ambulances kept arriving with wounded from the Brunete front. One of the Black ambulance drivers was Ted Gibbs, a man I known from Chicago's West Side. Seeing Gibbs in Spain wasn't a surprise for me. Like most of the men who went to Spain, Gibbs came out of the deep struggle of the Depression of the early thirties and was always in the thick of the battle for dignity for his people. Early the next morning, to complete my new assignment, I was on my way to Barcelona, driving a small Fiat car that had been captured on the southern front. My two passengers were from Poland; a doctor and a nurse on their way to search for some sorely needed medical supplies for the hospital.

When we reached Barcelona, they made their rounds of the city, leaving me free for several hours to roam the streets. I soon found myself walking down what is called the Great White Way, Las Ramblas. It was an unusual promenade, formed much like an island, by two narrow, long streets beginning at Plaza Catalonia, then slanting down nearly a mile, past a huge statue of Columbus, to the waterfront. Approaching a dock, I watched as a Russian vessel was being tugged to a dock where men waited to unload cargo being sent to Republican Spain.

I left the dock and walked slowly back up Las Ramblas. It was much like being in a park, with large trees shading the whole area. There were many bookstalls, newspaper stands and cafe tables in the center. The cafes themselves were on the far side of the street and the waiters had to cross the swiftly moving traffic to reach their customers on the island. Behind me I heard a loud squeak from an automobile. I turned in time to see a waiter regaining his poise, after a near miss, still holding onto his tray. But things got back to normal quickly. The waiter had not been harmed and the huge crowd continued to move peacefully along its way.

Just before I reached the Plaza Catalonia, I stopped dead. Then I felt embarrassed. I was doing something to others that often happened to me in Spain. People would stare at me because they had never seen a Black before. And now I was staring at two Blacks seated at a cafe table. I thought, they may be Cubans or Africans. I took a chance, not knowing what language they spoke. I strode over and said, "Hello."

The two men, both volunteers, had just arrived from New York. They introduced themselves as Charles Parker and Vernold Beebe. From them I was able to hear all of the recent news back home. After a conversation with them, which seemed altogether too short, I rushed off to meet the doctor and nurse.

It was after dark as I drove along the winding road at what I thought was a fast pace. The doctor seemed to be in a hurry. In a language I didn't understand he kept saying something that sounded like, "*Anda, anda!*" I assumed he was telling me, "Go faster, Go faster," so I pushed the gas pedal to the floor. Then we seemed to be flying. All at once, looming before us was a deadend. I yanked the wheel to the left to avoid the embankment. How we ever got out of having an accident I'll never know, but the doctor stopped yelling "*Anda, anda!*"

We arrived in the little resort town of Benicasim at one in the morning. I quickly unloaded the medical supplies and we were off to Valencia. The city had been bombed heavily earlier in the night, but now all was quiet. The sky over the city had a hazy yellow glow rising from the burning buildings.

I managed to get a few hours sleep before I was told that I would be driving three men to the town of Teruel. When I arrived at the hotel, which was called The Londres, the three men were waiting just in front. They introduced themselves as: Herbert Matthews, of *The New York Times,* Sefton Delmer, of the London *Daily Express,* and Ernest Hemingway. I almost couldn't believe that the great "Papa" would be one of my passengers.

I had never been in this part of Spain, but I soon found my way through the busy morning rush to a street that would take us out to the road that led to Teruel. The newspaperman from England was in front beside me. Matthews and Hemingway occupied the rear seat. I was as quiet as a mouse. After all, I had never chauffeured such distinguished company before. I listened eagerly and was soon able to discern who was speaking. Nevertheless, the conversation was difficult to understand because Matthews had a soft voice, until there was something with which he disagreed, and Hemingway's voice was gruff. Sometimes Delmer, the Englishman, would join the conversation. I found it almost impossible to understand him. It seemed as though he was speaking a foreign language. They talked about the war. At one point the conversation became so heated that Matthews exclaimed, "No more for the moment! I've had it for a while." Hemingway laughed, then began to talk about the bulls that had become a problem outside of Madrid. Formerly they were used in the bull-fights, but since the war there was no longer anyone to look after them and they had become wild.

They joked about Errol Flynn, and Hemingway told the story of Flynn taking the subway as close as he could to the fascist front line that ringed Madrid. Flynn had been able to see the puffs of smoke from the guns and the heavy artillery in the hills. As he stood there sightseeing, a bullet hit a man next to him in the jaw and another whisked past his ear.

"What? Near his ear? Did ol' Errol prove to be as brave as he always is in the movies?" asked Matthews.

"Well, let's not down the fellow. I understand he made several sizable donations to the Republican cause," Hemingway said and continued, "His swordsmanship might be suspect, but his pocketbook is on the right side!"

I hadn't said a word up to that time, but now I relaxed and joined the laughter at the Flynn story. I stopped laughing as I saw a donkey coming straight towards the car. I slammed on the brakes. The loud screech frightened the animal and it made a sudden turn. I missed it. Although the donkey had not been hit we were all a little shaken up. Hemingway casually suggested that we have a drink. Of course he was joking. We hadn't seen a town for miles.

Everybody was quiet now as we drove along a road that we were no longer certain would take us to Teruel. Hemingway directed me to stop so that he and Matthews could look over a road map. Hemingway, in his usual joking style, commented, "It would be a tragedy for a reporter from the *New York Times* to be captured by the fascist Franco, who already has that damn reporter Carney dispatching his lies to the *Times,* which they print regularly.

We were much closer to Teruel than we had realized. Within minutes we were driving in what had been the outskirts of the town. What a strange and sad feeling I had driving slowly through where the war had been. Eerie signs of a brutal battle could be seen: a single boot that once held a foot, part of a bloodstained uniform, all of the dead cats and dogs . . . It struck me suddenly that here Spaniards, Americans and other Internationals died in a most heroic fight to capture the town of Teruel.

Further down the road we parked where the main street met a deep trench. We got out of the car and walked up the red clay steps into the narrow street that looked as if it had been the principal shopping area. From the beginning of our walk, I noticed the smell of sour wine. Matthews, who at times would call Hemingway "Ernie," said, "Ernie, now you can have your drink." But it didn't really seem that funny. Matthews and Sefton Delmer began to take pictures of the ruins. Hemingway had his notebook out as if he had found something of great value for his book *For Whom The Bell Tolls.*

One of the only things still alive in town ran between my legs. A big rat the size of a cat! I yelled so loud that everybody ran for cover as if the fascists had reappeared to retake the town.

An hour or so later we started the journey back to Valencia. I was anxious to leave before dark, because I didn't want to use my headlights for fear that they might be seen by enemy planes. For the first few miles we were all rather quiet. They were all busy writing, when Matthews broke the silence by asking Sefton how he felt about the capture of Teruel. Sefton replied, "This is a victory for anti-fascist forces all over the world. If my country and France would do away with the embargo against Republican Spain and stopped their arms from going to the fascists, there would be no way that the Republicans could lose the war."

By the time we arrived back in Valencia I was dead tired and ready for bed. But I wasn't going to miss the invitation I received from the writers to have dinner with them. Three of us waited in the lobby while Matthews cabled his story to the paper. When he returned we all walked up a flight of stairs and entered the dining room where we seated ourselves at a table near the window overlooking the plaza. The table was covered with a linen tablecloth with a silver setting polished to a fine lustre. The menu was *calamares* (squid), as a starter, a Spanish dish I always passed up, but Hemingway seemed to relish the dish, especially with a fifth of scotch that appeared from nowhere. The main dish was *garbanzos* (chick peas) cooked in olive oil, served with a glass of house wine. Dessert was an orange compote.

Before the last course was served, Matthews made it clear that he wanted a true bull story, asking Hemingway to tell more about the wild bulls running around. So Hemingway obliged, talking about the wild bulls in Fuencarral Hills. He told how he got together with men in transport, a truckload of them, who had gone bull hunting. Two bulls were killed and a great feast was had by all. I liked the bull story. Hemingway had such a comical way of telling it. Then Delmer, the Englishman, had a story to tell. It was about the day he was in Madrid running around looking for transportation to the front. He didn't speak Spanish and couldn't understand a man who was trying to explain to him how he could reach the front. In exasperation, the man took him by the arm to the streetcar stop. "This will take you to the front lines," the man said in broken English. So, for the price of ten centavos, he got to the front lines. We all laughed. I thanked them for inviting me to dinner, and said good-bye. The only one of the three I would meet later was Herbert Matthews of the *Times*.

There was a message waiting for me that evening that my truck was ready to be picked up. I was overjoyed. It had taken two weeks to make the repair. The next morning I went over to the Auto-Park before the door was even open and told the lieutenant in charge that I was the one to pick up the Russian-made truck that belonged to the Thaelmann Battalion. He reached toward the board where the keys were usually hung, and the keys weren't there. Not only were there no keys, there was no truck. My truck had been "organized." In Spain, the expression "to organize," meant "to exchange," without the owner of the property being aware of the transaction. American cigarettes were frequently "organized" and replaced by French ones, although the concept of "exchange" was not limited to cigarettes. In Spain it was applied to guns, boots or anything that was not nailed down. I didn't know if tanks and planes were also being organized.

I walked around the streets near the Auto-Park hoping to spot the truck. No luck. The lieutenant at the Auto-Park phoned Albacete for further instructions. What was I going to tell them back at headquarters? First I had to find out where the Thaelmanns were now located. The lieutenant at the Auto-Park phoned Albacete for instructions. It was confirmed, as expected, that the Thaelmanns were no longer at Brunete. My instructions were to ride in the truck which would be carrying mail to the new front where the next battle was anticipated. I waited at the place from where the truck was supposed to leave at seven that evening.

It was still daylight when I climbed into the back of the open-bodied truck, where three Spanish men sat on crates. Standing beside the driver was a Spanish boy no more than twelve years old who could not be talked out of going to the front. Another man, wearing civilian clothes, climbed into the truck and took a seat alongside me. Much to my surprise, it was Langston Hughes.

Langston Hughes was one of America's best known poets. He had come to Spain as a reporter for the *Afro-American,* a major Black newspaper which was and still is published in Baltimore and in Washington, D.C. Now I was happy that my truck had been "organized." Langston wanted me to tell him about my duties in Spain.

"I'm with the Thaelmanns. I drive a truck."

"Oh, you must have been in Brunete", he responded with interest.

"I was there all right." As I was about to tell him about the battle, the driver pulled the truck to one side of the road, climbed down, and walked back to talk with the young boy. I couldn't understand all he was saying to the young lad, but he must have been trying to dissuade him from going to the front. Whatever was said, the young boy remained in the truck while the driver climbed back into his seat and we continued on our way. Maybe the boy had taken a line from that hymn, *"Si tu descea comer bien viene a la fronta Guadalajara* (If you want to eat well, come to the front at Guadalajara)."

As the truck made its way through the darkness across the Spanish countryside, Langston Hughes and I exchanged information about many of the Black members of the Abraham Lincoln Brigade and about the battle at Brunete. I told him all I knew, beginning with Vaughan Love, from Dayton, Tennessee, who referred to the battle at Brunete as "the twenty-one days of hell."

Hughes told me about some of the Black combatants with whom he had spoken. Walter Garland commanded a machine gun company. Luchell McDaniels was nicknamed "El Fantastico" by the Spaniards, because of his ability to throw a grenade with either hand. Morris Wickman of Philadelphia was killed during the first days of the action.

Langston took out his notebook and leafed through it for reference while he told me about some of the volunteers with whom he had been speaking; Douglas Roach, Ralph Thornton, Harry Haywood, Louise Thompson and Frank Warfield.

When we were about a mile from Teruel the truck driver made a stop. The temperature had dropped sharply and it grew very chilly in spite of it being August. Noting a slight tremor in Langston's voice, I pulled the blanket out of my pack and placed it around his shoulders. The little Spanish boy and the two other soldiers had covered themselves with a piece of canvas and were all sound asleep. Langston and I continued our conversation, but the temperature continued to drop. When I began to feel like it must be about zero, I placed a canvas over my shoulders.

Langston Hughes asked me if I knew Abraham Lewis. When Abe first came to Spain he was attached to a transport regiment and within two months he was made a sergeant. Soon he went on to become quartermaster-in-charge of the training base for English-speaking soldiers. There he was responsible for the feeding, clothing, sanitation and recreational facilities for the entire base.

Few International Brigaders who came to Spain wanted to serve as cooks. They wanted to fight. Consequently, Spanish cooks had to be introduced to the ways of cooking in different countries. A school was set up in which the first thing that the cooks were taught was how to read in their own language. This was a most significant step in a country like Spain with its appalling illiteracy.

It was three o'clock in the morning when we reached our destination at the Aragon front. The front stretched from Teruel, along the mountains, across dry hills and barren plains, all the way to the French border. The Thaelmann and other Internationals were preparing for the next offensive. Two men from the Thaelmann Brigade were there to meet us and to pick up the mail. After saying good-bye to Langston Hughes I watched him as he walked away with my blanket still over his shoulders. He was wearing a thin summer suit and needed the blanket more than I did.

My two German comrades and I carried the heavy mailbags up a long steep donkey trail. At the top was an open plain where the staff of the Thaelemann Brigade was huddled around a bonfire. I didn't understand why it was that they laughed when I started to explain to them about the loss of my truck. Then they told me that it was here. Gaffer, the German comrade with only one arm, had organized my truck by mistake and had driven it to the front.

That same night, having had no rest, I started off once again in my own truck on the return journey to Albacete. By three in the morning I was so overcome with fatigue that I could no longer keep my eyes open. I pulled up and stopped under a tree with branches large enough to provide camouflage for the truck. In spite of the bitter cold, I soon fell asleep. I must have slept for several hours, because when I was awakened by the drone of a plane headed in my direction, I was surprised by the bright sunlight. Uncertain as to whether I had been spotted by the enemy pilot, I could do nothing but wait. When the plane finally turned away, I drove at a high speed toward Valencia. I remember starting down the road. I knew I had seen the plane. I heard the groan of bombers as they approached. But whatever happened then, I will never know. I lost all connection with the world. The next forty-eight hours will be forever missing from my life.

Chapter 9

Going Home

I had been brought into the hospital nearly half dead. When I opened my eyes, a Polish woman doctor, also a volunteer, was standing over me. She told me that, apart from being very badly shaken, and in a state of shock, there was no specific diagnosis to be made for my condition. I was the only American in the small hospital located in Orihuela, near the coastal city of Alicante. I was told, however, about the many wounded American volunteers who had been brought here from the battlefield when the fighting had been taking place on the Aragon front.

Many weeks passed before I was able to get around with the aid of a cane. It was a mellow afternoon almost three months after I had been brought into the hospital. The sun was warm and pleasant. A bird was singing in the olive trees. I sat on the sunny side of a white building along with the other wounded. On this day the nurse walked directly over to me. She took my pulse. "How are you feeling today?" she said.

"Fine . . . good." I watched her carefully for clues as to what she was thinking.

"Very good, but remember not to overdo it." That she left without taking the pulse of the other men seemed rather strange to me.

The next morning at bed check the same nurse came up to me again and said, "You'll be going to Albacete today."

"Why?"

"I don't know," and she took my pulse again.

I was taken to Albacete along with several other soldiers who had also been wounded. Some were on crutches and some had arms in slings. We stopped at the hospital in Murcia to pick up still more volunteers who had been wounded.

Upon arrival in Albacete, I was taken to the office of William Lawrence, who was in charge of the American volunteers. As he greeted me warmly, I could tell that he was observing my movements carefully. He caught me by surprise when he announced to me, "You're going home!"

"Why?" I demanded. "The war is not over."

"Comrade, the doctors tell me it will be months before you can fight again. You can better serve the cause of Spain back home. You know our government didn't approve of our coming to Spain to fight fascism. This will be a way of testing what will happen when other men and women return home."

It seemed as though nothing could be worse than the news that I would have to go home. But then Lawrence took a letter from his desk drawer and handed it to me. It was addressed to me. "It's from your mother." The letter said that my grandmother was dead. Grandma dead? I couldn't believe it. My ninety-six-year-old grandmother, who had been a slave, died while I was on the battlefields of Spain.

The telephone rang and while Lawrence was answering the call I sat thinking about my grandmother and of going home. The door opened and in walked James Ford, the highest-ranking American Communist to visit Spain. In 1932 he had run for Vice President of the United States along with Earl Browder, who ran for President. James Ford and I talked while waiting for Lawrence's telephone conversation to end. Ford gave me strength by saying, "You will be very valuable at home, helping to alert the American people to the danger of fascism and organizing them to work for the cause of Spain."

James Ford was not the only leading Communist who visited Spain. There were also Jacques Duclos and Andre Marty both Communist leaders in France. Marty was a founder and an important figure in the International Brigades.

When Lawrence finished talking on the telephone, I stayed for a while, listening to Ford tell about his meeting with La Pasionaria, Dolores Ibarruri, another great leader. When Frank Feingersh, another volunteer, walked into the office, Lawrence introduced us and told us that we would be going home together. Frank and I then went together to a cafe in the center of Albacete. Over a cup of coffee we began to talk about our battle experiences.

Later on we decided to take advantage of what might be our last opportunity to see a bullfight. The bullfighting went on in Spain, war or no war. I was reminded of those Sundays that Admiral Kilpatrick and I spent together when we worked at the Auto-Park. After the bullfight, to show off a bit, I took Frank to the same hotel where Kilpatrick and I used to go and have our Sunday *arroz con pollo* (chicken and rice).

The next day, Monday, we were ready for our long trip home. While we waiting at the little sidewalk cafe for the truck which would take us to Barcelona, a young Black man named James Holt Peck came around. He looked no more than eighteen and was dressed in a smart uniform, different from what I had seen at the front. Peck was one of the two Black American volunteers who had flown in the Republican Air Force. The other was Paul Williams. Peck told us he and Williams had sailed from the Port of New York on the liner *Queen Elizabeth* in 1937. On the same ship and also headed for Spain were two American authors, Dorothy Parker and Lillian Hellman. Their passports were not good for travel to Spain, because of the United States embargo, so they landed in France.

Peck and Williams's first stop on Spanish soil was the town of Figueras, where they were housed in the same old fort where I had stayed. Both had commercial licenses to fly, but being Black, their flying careers had been frustrated by the limited number of Black pilots in the United States—a grand total of five by the 1930's.

When the Italian fascists invaded Ethiopia in October, 1935, only one or two Black fliers were able to join the Ethiopian Air Force in their fight against the Italians. It was the same Italian Air Force that had bombed huts in Ethiopia, killing thousands of old people and children, that were now flying with Franco's Air Force in Spain.

Thirty-one American pilots in all volunteered to fly with the Republican Air Force in Spain. Other pilots came from countries such as England, France and Russia. The Russian fliers who came to Spain startled the military attaches of the world by introducing their new plane, the Pilikarpov, a monoplane. Peck told me that he met the Russian pilots during his third week of training and that they had said they were in Spain primarily in an advisory capacity. In little less than four months of combat Peck shot down five planes. He also became friends with Ernest Hemingway. They used to have lunch together in Valencia, the new provisional capital. Peck said of Hemingway, "He truly believed in the Republic, and was one of its unselfish supporters, giving generously of his time, money and prestige to the war against fascism."

Patrick Roosevelt was another Black pilot, but it was never possible for him to fly in Spain. Only a few days before his arrival the Spanish government ordered the air force to begin using newly trained Spanish pilots instead of Internationals, so Pat joined the Abraham Lincoln Brigade just at the time it was poised for a major attack on the fascist armies all along the Ebro. I had read in the *Volunteer* that Pat had been wounded. One day when I was driving past the town of Tarragona I stopped by the hospital to see him. During that visit Pat told me about how the Lincoln's had faced a large enemy force in the Sierra del Pandolls. A see-saw battle ensued in which the mountain ridges changed hands as much as five times a day. Pat was hit by a bullet in the leg and was taken across the Ebro to a hospital in Tarragona. He also laughed, "There is a joke going around the hospital about me. The doctor told the nurses to notify him at once if they saw wounds turning black. And the nurses wanted to know how they could tell when my wound turned black."

Before Pat could finish his story a young Black medical student named Thaddeus Battle, from Howard University, walked into the ward. A quiet-mannered man who wore glasses, he had become an ambulance driver. We all began to speak about our various experiences in the war.

Battle described what he had seen of the destruction of large sections of Madrid. Schools, libraries and University City, which was a multimillion-dollar educational center, were all in ruins. He said, "The fascists tear down that which it has taken people years to build."

■ ■ ■

Nine of us left Albacete by truck for Barcelona. A young man, Louis Lefkowitz, mailman of the Internationals in Madrid, was picked up on the way. We arrived in Barcelona at five in the afternoon, just before the sun set. We had more than six hours in which to eat and to take a last stroll along Las Ramblas before our train was to leave.

At exactly ten o'clock, one hour before our train was scheduled to leave, all hell broke loose. Italian bombers that had been based on the island of Majorca flew overhead in droves. We wondered if we would get to go home or if we would be among the many victims killed that night by the bombs dropped by the fascists. We were lucky. When things eventually quieted down we made our way to the railroad station, only to find gaping holes where bombs had made direct hits. The bomb squad was already out there digging.

The train that would take us to France had been spared from a direct hit, although all its windows had been shattered.

It was still dark when we pulled out of the train station headed for France. A chilling wind blew off the Pyrenees and right through our windowless train. The Mediterranean was filled with Italian gunboats. Sitting on the train, too cold to sleep, I had plenty of time to ponder my departure from Spain. The war was still to be won. What about my comrades who must still carry on the fight? I remembered my dead friends—Alonzo Watson, Oliver Law, Milton Herndon and so many comrades from the German Thaelmann Battalion. They would remain in Spain forever. I wondered about those who had been captured. During the first few months of the war Franco's army had standing orders to execute any Internationals captured. But things had changed. After the Republicans captured a large number of German and Italian fliers, the fascist High Command issued orders that all Internationals should be taken alive for exchange.

Among the ninety or more Americans who had been captured, there were three Blacks. Thomas Brown was from St. Louis, Missouri. Claude Pringle from the Ohio Valley was a coal miner and a World War I veteran. Edward Johnson of Columbus, Ohio, was another World War I veteran. He had taken part in the National Hunger March of 1932, when thousands of hungry, jobless veterans and their families were attacked, at the command of President Hoover, within sight of the White House, by General Douglas MacArthur's troops. Johnson, after repatriation, told friends in Columbus that he had been tortured while in prison and that some of the other prisoners who were non-political before their capture became over-politicized as a result of their prison experiences.

It was not until more than year after my return from Spain that the surviving prisoners crossed the International Bridge to freedom at Hendaye at two in the afternoon on April 22, 1939. At the moment of his release Edward Johnson was told by a fascist officer, "If I had my way, I would shoot every one of you."

■ ■ ■

When the ten of us arrived in Paris we were still dressed in our battle outfits. The French Trade Union of Paris supplied new suits for our return home. Little has been said or written about the role played by the French people as host to thousands, or possibly tens of thousands of volunteers who spent days, sometimes weeks, in France during the duration of the Spanish Civil War.

The ship on which I returned to New York docked at the same place from which I had set sail. The tourist passengers were allowed to leave the ship, but we were detained by the FBI. All of us were huddled into a small room of the ship, awaiting our fate. These FBI men, sitting and pondering what to do with us, looked and acted as if they would have been more comfortable with the fascists we had been fighting in Spain. But we had faced worse: bullets and exploding bombs. To complete our assignment we came home to test the climate, to see what would happen to others returning home from Spain. An FBI agent looked at me with bafflement. It seemed as if he wanted to ask what a boy from Mississippi was doing fighting a war in Spain.

One hour passed. Were they waiting for word from Washington? Finally we were told we could leave the ship. They took our passports and we asked when they would be returned to us. All the FBI agent said was, "We'll see." It took a US Supreme Court decision, the Paul Robeson case and the restoration of his right to travel, before we, too, could go outside of our country again.

As we emerged from the ship, singing and shouting, we saw the many people who had come to the dock to greet us. People lifted signs of welcome into the air and there were cries of, *"No pasaran!"* The radio and the press maneuvered to get to us. The crowd embraced us and kissed us and shook our hands. Relatives of some of the veterans wept joyfully. So many of us had been killed, it gladdened hearts to see that some of us were still alive.

It took hours for those who had organized a place for us to stay to free us from the crowd. We were taken to the Hotel Grand which was located around Thirty-third Street and Broadway. It was a small, clean, modest-looking hotel.

Several of the men had signed for their rooms, but when my turn came the clerk didn't even seem to look at me. "Sorry," he said. "No vacancy."

One of the organizers stepped forward, frowning. "But I thought you had plenty of rooms." The clerk still looked straight through me. "No vacancy," he repeated.

"No vacancy? Or is it that you don't rent to Negroes?"

The clerk's tone couldn't have been more indifferent; it remained as stonily unmoved as that of the man who'd stopped Elijah Collins many years ago at the Meridian, Mississippi, train station. I said, *"No Vacancy!"*

Inwardly I winced. So soon? I had hardly left the boat and here it was. After having experienced being welcomed in cafes and hotels in Spain and France, I was doubly shocked to be hit so quickly. The pain went as deeply as any bullet could have done. I had the dizzy feeling I was back in the trenches again. But this was another front. I was home.

I was not ready for anyone to tell me that I *must* go to Harlem for a hotel, regardless of the fact that it was the one place that I loved most. I had often wondered, while in Spain, if I would ever walk its streets again.

My comrades did exactly what I expected of them. They immediately picked up their belongings and left the hotel. Eventually we found rooms in Greenwich Village.

Nevertheless, it was difficult to accept that there existed flea-bag hotels with petty clerks that would give me such a humiliating welcome back to America. This was another kind of warfare. When the attacks hurt and are like being hit by a bullet, I must find ways to strike back. It isn't feasible to use a gun. I had grown tougher. Nothing, not even the threat of death, could force me back into the role of saying "Yassuh."

Some days there would be defeats; other days, victories. And in between times, advances, retreats, attacks and counterattacks. But I could be sure of one thing: the enemy could not win forever. As sure as the sun rises, people will keep rising and keep fighting for human dignity and freedom.

Chapter 10

After Spain

Once back in the United States, I settled down in New York. Pat Roosevelt and I shared an apartment for a while down on the East Side, on Ninth Street. Pat set up a radio repair shop in one room, and we had a coal-burning stove. That was a bad time for us. At one point, in order to eat, we had to borrow money from Huddie Leadbetter, better known as "Leadbelly," and his wife Martha. We had met Leadbelly at the Village Vanguard where he played his famous twelve string guitar.

But it wasn't too long before I was in the United States Army, along with five or six hundred other Spanish Civil War vets. I joined up to fight Hitler in World War II. At that time the army was still segregated. I went through basic training for the Signal Corps but was pulled out of my outfit when it went overseas. I was the only one to be pulled out. A lieutenant told me he believed it was because of my participation in the Spanish Civil War. I became a one-man detail, shipped to Utah, where I was in charge of a unit doing dirty work for the medics at Bushnell Army Hospital. The last straw came when I was sent to the dental clinic for a simple tooth extraction. An infection set in which hospitalized me for three months until I was honorably discharged.

Having served in the army qualified me to have my college tuition paid for under the GI Bill. After having earned a degree in electronics at the RCA Institute, I worked as a technician. Because of my political involvement, during the McCarthy era finding a job became increasingly difficult. I was harassed by the FBI and rejected from every job for which I applied. Never in my wildest imagination had I considered becoming self-employed or an entrepreneur, but finding no employment, I was finally forced to set up my own TV repair shop. In addition to my work as a technician, I continued to be deeply involved in the struggle for justice. From 1964-1968 I served as President of the Greenwich Village–Chelsea chapter of the NAACP. During that time our branch sent tons of food and clothing to Mississippi. At the height of the struggle, when people were putting their lives on the line, three members of our branch went to Meridian, Mississippi, just twenty-four miles from my home town of Quitman.

■ ■ ■

It was some thirty years after leaving Spain that I decided to write a book which would reflect the Black experience in the Spanish Civil War. To refresh my memory I wanted to talk with the seven or eight Black volunteers who were still alive. Although I had not seen either of them in twenty years, I was able to find Tom Page and Barney Rucker without too much difficulty. Tom was one of the few Internationals who had served with the Ninety-Sixth Division, a Spanish outfit. He fought at Brunete, Belchite, Teruel, and the Ebro. Amidst our reminiscing about Spain, Tom said, "I remember how sometimes a whole town would turn out when they heard there was a Black man around. Spain was the first place that I ever felt like a free man. If someone didn't like you, they told you that to your face. It had nothing to do with the color of your skin."

Tom told me about his experience in the US Army during World War II. He was sent to Italy where he was assigned to a work gang crushing rocks which would be used to make roads. I told him, "Hell, with your combat experience, they should have made you a company commander!"

It was on a bitter cold January day that I took a bus to Orange, New Jersey, to visit Barney Rucker and his wife, Helen. Over a beer we talked about Spain. Barney and I recalled that night we had spent together in the subway in Madrid. Barney then told me about his departure from Spain. He was among the last to leave in late October 1938, and had to climb across the Pyrenees to France. Barney explained, "Hitler was already on the march and when we arrived in Paris things were in an uproar. There were soldiers everywhere. Americans were fleeing Europe and it was not easy to get passage out.

It had been a long time since I had last seen Pat Roosevelt. Originally he was from Seattle, Washington, but after Spain Pat stayed on the East Coast. He lived for twenty-seven years in Corona, Queens, on the bottom floor of a simple two story clapboard house. He had a TV service shop. When I asked Pat what he had been doing during the thirties, those years of the Great Depression, he replied, "Trying to live. You know, I was a commercial pilot then. Many people were building their own planes and they would call on me to try them out. I went to Spain because I wanted to fly."

After my visit with Pat we stayed in contact until his death in 1981. When I learned that money had to be raised for his burial, tears streamed down my cheeks.

■ ■ ■

Every since returning from Spain my passport was withheld from me by the US government. Finally, as a result of the decision in the Paul Robeson case, I was able in 1971 to again obtain a passport and to travel outside of the US. I decided to make a trip to Europe on a Yugoslav freighter. It would be a good way to start writing. The journey from New York to Riejecka, Yugoslavia, lasted twenty-six days, during which time we sailed in the Mediterranean Sea off the coast of Spain. I wondered how I could come to Europe and not visit Spain, the place where for the first time in my life I experienced what it was to be a free man. Whether or not to return to Spain was not an easy decision to make. After all, it was still a fascist country ruled by Franco. I decided, nevertheless, to go to Spain for a two week visit.

I took a midnight train out of Paris. About daybreak the train arrived in Marseilles. When I looked at the small map of France which I carried with me, it appeared that it would not be long before I would once again be in Spain. A hot and cold feeling overcame me when I considered what might happen to an enemy of Franco. By the time the train reached Perpignan, a small city located about thirty miles from the Spanish border, I had decided to get off in order to give myself time to reconsider. I took a room in a small hotel and slept for a few hours. Later, in a small cafe where I went to have dinner, I was surprised to hear the people all around me speaking Spanish. Listening to them talk I realized that I could understand much of what was being said. I beckoned to a man at the next table, then greeted him in Spanish. I asked, "Are you from Spain?" to which he answered, *"Si, si."*

"How long have you lived in France?" When he answered, "Ever since the end of the Spanish Civil War," I knew he was just the person I had been looking for. I began by telling him that I was one of the Americans who had fought in Spain with the Abraham Lincoln Brigade. His eyes bulged and he began to beckon to others to come over. Everyone in the cafe was standing around my table and to my surprise they began to ask me about people. "Do you know Steve Nelson?" "Where is Wolff?" "What has happened to Salaria Kee, the Black nurse?" They talked about the aid sent by the Lincolns, after they returned to the US, to the thousands of Spaniards who crossed the border to escape Franco. I asked for their advice, "Is it all right to visit Spain?" They assured me there would be no problem.

The next day I continued on my journey. Our first stop was the border town of Port Bou, where all train passengers were required to go through customs. Everywhere I looked there were police in their green uniforms and black three-cornered hats. No doubt there were just as many plain-clothes police too. After clearing customs we boarded another train which moved slowly over the same tracks that I rode over when I left Spain forty years earlier. There were differences. This time the train windows were intact and no Italian gunboats waited in the Mediterranean to shell the train.

As we approached the outskirts of Barcelona, I began to see the horrors the war had wrought. Miles of empty buildings stood as though they were official monuments to the war. The train rolled into the same station that had suffered a heavy bombing the night I left for home.

I took my heavy suitcase from the rack and carried it as I made my way down the long walk to the large iron gate leading to the waiting room. As I approaching the gate one of many tall men who were standing around lunged at my bag. I was shocked, but then suddenly realized he was saying, "Taxi, taxi."

"Si, si hombre." He led me to the taxi stand. I climbed into a taxi and told the driver, "hotel," and made him understand it must not be an expensive one. To my surprise the man who led me to the taxi climbed in beside me. Having a private porter accompany me to an inexpensive hotel was a new experience for me. Seeing thousands of poor people walking the streets, it all became clear to me. There were no jobs and this was a way to make a few pesos.

The taxi deposited me at a hotel just off Las Ramblas. It cost only a dollar and a half a day. There I was given a clean room. Looking out the window at the hundreds of people strolling up and down Las Ramblas I realized that none of them were standing in groups and talking as they used to do before Franco.

Late that afternoon, just before sunset, I took a stroll and then sat on a bench overlooking the Plaza Catalonia. Standing all around the plaza were the officers in green with their machine guns. As I walked to my hotel along the back streets I saw armored trucks waiting as though ready for action.

At three o'clock in the morning on my third night in Spain I was awakened by screams from a man who I could only presume was being tortured just a few rooms away from mine. There was no way I could sleep the rest of that night. I was experiencing just a little of what life under the fascist regime was like. I wanted to leave the hotel, but doubted if it would be any different in another one.

I decided to leave Barcelona, but had to wait for the arrival of an important letter which I was expecting from Paris. I had been checking for mail each morning at the American Express and was relieved when I found that my letter had at last arrived. Then my worst dream came true. The German woman who was in charge of the mail said, "Wait, I have something else for you." I heard something falling and ringing like marbles hitting the floor. It turned out to be buttons that said *"Free Angela Davis."*

Before coming on this trip I had been working for the release of Angela Davis from prison. So, I decided when making my plans for the trip that it would be a good idea to bring along a suitcase of Angela Davis buttons to distribute in Europe. Having run out of the buttons I ordered more and requested that they be sent to me at the American Express in Paris. I left word there that only letters should be forwarded to me in Spain —no packages. Now here were the buttons. They had been forwarded to me here by mistake. My first thought was, "Oh Lord, what is this. Here I am in fascist Spain with Angela Davis buttons. What if this gets reported to the authorities?" All the while walking back to the hotel I wondered what to do with the buttons. Then I pulled myself together. I had faced Franco before in the Civil War forty years ago. I spent the rest of the day sitting on many benches and somehow leaving a button behind at each one. By sundown all of the buttons were gone.

■ ■ ■

The scenery on the bus trip from Barcelona to Valencia was very beautiful, just as it had been in 1937. The orange groves still stretched down to the sea on one side of the road and up to the mountains on the other side. However, there were differences. Then, at every stop a crowd would gather to greet us and give us gifts of oranges —the only thing they had to give. Now there were many roadblocks. Visitors were treated respectfully, but the natives were detained and given a good-going over. All papers had to be in order.

Once in Valencia, I found a hotel where I rested for a few hours before going for dinner. In the hotel bar I met some soccer (called "football" in Spain) players. Franco gave one thing to the people of Spain: support for sports. The main sport in Spain is "football". It is also the main topic of conversation. This is a clever trick to keep the people from thinking about the government. The "football" players I met that evening were from Orihuela. When they asked where I was from I told them, and said I had been in Orihuela before, but was pleased they did not ask me when that had been. As much as I wanted to, there was no way I could have told them that it was during the Spanish Civil War.

After speaking in Spanish with the "football" players, I was surprised to hear English being spoken. I turned

around and saw four Black women seated at a table. They
were pleased to have me join them, and I ordered a round
of drinks. When the women told me they were from Ohio,
I said, "I have a friend in New York who is from the Mid-
west, but I don't know where."

"Walter Garland."

One of the women, whose name was Sarah, spoke up
and said, "I know his wife. She and I belong to the same
club." Oh, what a glowing feeling overcame me when I
knew I was about to learn the whereabouts of my friend
Walter. It was like a knife had entered my heart when she
said, "Walter died two years ago." I could not hold back my
tears. We all mourned together.

The next morning, while walking in the park, I saw an
old man with a walking stick sitting on a bench. I thought
to myself that perhaps it would be possible to talk with
him. All of the Spanish people I had attempted to talk with
were polite but uncommunicative. As I sat down next to
him on the bench, I said, *"Buenas dias."* Then I was silent
for a while before I asked, "Are you from Valencia?"

"No. I am from Bilbao, in the north of Spain." He went
on to tell me that he was a retired railroad worker and had
moved south for the warmer climate.

"How are things here in Spain?" I enquired. To which
he replied, "Bad, bad," and within the next few moments
he got up and walked away. I couldn't blame the people
for not talking with anyone they did not know well. Franco
had the prisons filled. People with no criminal record
received sentences of forty years. Their crime was that they
had fought in the Republican army.

Shortly after the old man left I resumed my walk and
searched for some of the places I had known in the city
forty years earlier. For a while I was completely lost. Then I
came across a familiar well where people were still coming
to fill their buckets and jugs, just as their forbears had
done for centuries. From there I was able to find my way
to the old railroad station, which had remained the same

as I remembered it. Just behind it was the bullfight stadium, which also had not changed. From there I walked to the main part of town where I rested in one of the outdoor cafes.

The next morning I headed by train to Madrid. As the train wound its way slowly around the steep mountain curves, I saw two church steeples and a few chimneys still standing amidst the pine trees, reminders of the villages that had been destroyed by Hitler's bombers.

After four hours of traveling slowly through the hills and past steep gorges, the train picked up a bit of speed as we traveled across flat farmland. A roadway ran parallel to the train tracks just as it had during the war when we conveyed food to the millions of people in Madrid while the city was under siege. The deep trenches that had been dug then to give us some protection were now almost all covered with trees. Looking now beyond the trenches, I watched the peasants as they harvested wheat. Forty years ago they had toiled in those same fields in full view of the low-flying enemy planes.

I had planned to stay in Madrid for a few days, but a few hours was enough for me. German influence on the Spanish culture seemed to have destroyed it. Most of the people I saw were elderly Germans. In the dining room of the hotel where I stayed overnight, even Spanish food had been removed from the menu. I longed for some *garbanzos* and for *arroz con pollo*.

Leaving Madrid I caught a glimpse of the cemetery where many of the Internationals were buried. I sadly recalled bringing the body of one of the Germans from the Thaelmann Brigade here. He had been killed in the battle of Brunete.

The first stop the train was to make was at El Escorial, which had been the headquarters for my battalion. Through the train window I could see off to the right a monument which had been built by Franco in honor of the fascists who died in the Civil War. To the left was a road sign pointing to Brunete. Oh, what a feeling came over me knowing that just nearby were lying for all time the bones of the Americans and other Internationals who had died in the struggle for freedom in Spain.

As the train pulled out of El Escorial, I saw once more the ancient burial place of Spanish kings and nobility. It had not been bombed, although the towns and villages surrounding it were completely destroyed. I had never before experienced such silence on a train. I read a newspaper and glanced up occasionally at a man who stood at the door of our compartment that held six people. I could sense the fear of the Spanish people around me, for whom this train journey could be their last opportunity to escape Spain's fascist government.

When we arrived at the border town of San Sebastian, everyone had to show their travel documents. There was no way of knowing who would be detained. As the train started up again and moved into France, a storm of loud cheers broke out. Passengers got out the guitars and castanets that they had tucked away, and there was music and gaiety all the way to Paris.

Epilogue

In October of 1986, 120 veterans of the Abraham Lincoln Brigade, along with their families and friends, gathered in Madrid along with Internationals from twenty-five other countries. It was eleven years after the death of Franco. We had been invited by the democratic government of Spain for a fiftieth anniversary celebration.

The sun was shining as thousands of people poured into the Palacio de Congresos. All of the seats were taken and the aisles were filled as the ceremony got underway. The program included Spain's greatest performing artists. Among the writers, flamenco dancers, singers and guitarists were Antonio Gades, the famous dancer and choreographer, and Rafael Alberti, Spain's greatest living poet. All had come to pay homage to the International Brigaders.

That evening the moon rose over a peaceful Madrid, so very different from how it had been fifty years earlier when thousands of people made their way each evening to the subway to take shelter from the bombings. Now we headed for Retiro Park where the Mayor of Madrid, Juan Barraneu, welcomed us.

The next morning we were invited to meet with the beloved Dolores Ibarruri (La Pasionaria). Her fiery voice had galvanized Republican Spain in the struggle against

173

fascism that had captured the world's imagination. When the International Brigaders left Spain fifty years ago she had told us, "When the olive tree of peace puts forth its leaves again, entwined with the laurels of the Spanish Republic's victory—Come back!" Now I told her, "Pasionaria, we are here!"

After a week of festivities and celebrations in Madrid, we went on a bus tour which enabled us to visit the battlefields as well as Barcelona and Valencia. In the little town of Gandesa we participated in the dedication of a memorial to the thousands of brave volunteers who fought and gave their lives.

A ceremony was held at Villanueva Pardillo in honor of Oliver Law. Standing on a hillside overlooking a lovely green valley, Commander Steve Nelson said, "The world hardly took notice at the time that among this group of people who came from the US to fight to preserve democracy in Spain there were Black people, and they were treated as equals, and advanced on the basis of their ability. Oliver Law was selected by myself and others to command because he was the best man for the job. We didn't say much at the time, but it is important that we recognize now that it was an historic moment—a Black man was placed in charge of a largely white unit for the first time in US history. We want the world to share in the pride that we feel."

OFFICE OF THE MAYOR

CITY OF CHICAGO

HAROLD WASHINGTON
MAYOR

P R O C L A M A T I O N

WHEREAS, this year marks the 50th Anniversary of the entrance of the Abraham Lincoln Brigade as volunteers in defense of democracy in the Spanish Civil War; and

WHEREAS, over 200 Chicagoans joined this international movement to stop the spread of fascism; and

WHEREAS, Oliver Law, a leader of movements for relief of the poor and for political rights for Blacks and working people in Chicago in the early 1930's, was a commander in the Abraham Lincoln Brigade, thus becoming the first Black American to lead an integrated military force in the history of the United States; and

WHEREAS, the long-neglected historical significance of Oliver Law is being recognized in a program on November 21, 1987, sponsored by the Veterans of the Abraham Lincoln Brigade and the 50th Anniversary Committee, which will honor the continuing legacy of international solidarity represented by Oliver Law and the Abraham Lincoln Brigade:

NOW, THEREFORE, I, Harold Washington, Mayor of the City of Chicago, do hereby proclaim November 21, 1987, to be OLIVER LAW AND ABRAHAM LINCOLN BRIGADE DAY IN CHICAGO and urge all citizens to be cognizant of the special events arranged for this time and the importance of this history.

Dated this 18th day of November, 1987.

Mayor

Eighty-three of the Black volunteers from North America
known to have served in the Spanish Civil War

Alexander, Frank Edward
Archer, Amos
Baker, William
Battle, Thaddeus Arrington
Beebe, Vernold
Brown, Tom
Callion, Walter
Carter, Council Gibson
Chesterton
Chisholm, Albert Edward
Chowan, Mike
Cleveland, Roland
Coad, Mack
Cobbs, Walter
Collado, Tomas
Collins, Leroy
Cox, James
Cueria y Orbit, Basilio
Dicks, Walter
Dickson, Nathaniel
Donaowa, Arnold Bennett
Dukes, Larry Stratford
Frankson, Kanute (Oliver)
Garland, Walter Banjamin
Gavin, Eugene Victor
George, Henry
Gibbs, Theodore
Goldwyn, Gerald
Graham, Meredith Sydnor
Gutierrez, Centurio

Haywood, Harry
Harvey, George
Herndon, Milton
Hunter, John P.
Hunter, Oscar Henry
Jackson, Burt Edward
Johnson, Aaron Bernard
Johnson, Edward
Johnson, Richard
Kee, Salaria
Kilpatrick, Admiral
Law, Oliver
Lewis, Abraham
Lewis, Charles
Lisberg, Norman
Love, Vaughn
McDaniels, Eluard Luchell
Mitchell, Andrew
Moore, William
Morgan, Crawford
Page, Thomas.
Parker, Charles Augustus
Peck, James Lincoln Holt
Pringle, Claude
Prowell, Alpheus Danforth
Ransom, Marcus
Reeves, Otto
Rhetta, Virgil
Roach, Douglas
Roberson, James

Rochester, Sterling
Rodriguez, Julius
Roosevelt, Patrick
Rose, Oliver Charles
Rosario, Conrado Figueros
Rucker, Bernard
Seacord, Douglas
Swanson, Weat
Taylor, Joseph
Thornton, Ralph
Trent, Tom
Verdier, Herbert

Warfield, Frank
Waters, George Walter
Watson, Alonzo
Weiderman, Jefferson
White, Edward
Wickman, Morris Henry
Williams, Fred
Williams, Paul E.
Willis, Sam
Yates, James
Youngblood, Charles

Abolitionists, 113
Abraham Lincoln Brigade, 116, 118,
    120-22, 126, 131, 137, 150, 156, 166
Abyssinian Baptist Church, 90
Afro-American Newspaper, 150
Africa, 17, 27, 57, 86, 91, 94
Alabama, 17, 29
Albacete, 114-16, 123-24, 126, 128,
    133, 141-42, 149, 152, 154, 157
Albert Hotel, 88
Alberti, Rafael, 173
Alexander, Frank Edward, 176
Alicante, 116, 153
Alligator Swamp, 30
Almeria, 124
American Express, 168
American Federation of Labor (AFL),
    76, 92
American Medical Bureau, 128
Ansley, Ala., 31
Apollo, 86
Aragon Front, 120, 125, 127, 143, 151
Archer, Amos, 176
Archusa Creek, 15
Arles, France, 108
Armstrong, Louis, 29, 48
Arnold, Lester, 77, 79-83
Atkinson, Brooks, 133
Atlanta, Ga, 89
Atlanta University, 91
Auto-Park, 123-25, 128, 131, 143, 149,
    155

Baker, Josephine, 105
Baker, William, 176
Baltimore, Md., 150
Barcelona, 143-44, 155, 157, 167-69,
    174
Barraneu, Juan, 173
Basque, 122
Battle, Thaddeus Arrington, 157, 176
Beebe, Vernold, 145, 176
Belchite, 127, 164
Benchley, Robert, 133
Benicasim, 143, 145
Berlin, 132
Bessie, 59-77, 89
Bilbo, Theodore Gilmore, 27, 93, 96,
    119
Bilbao, 170

Birmingham, Ala., 30-33
Blakeney, Thomas, 18-20, 38, 57, 91
Bola, Okla., 17
Boston, Mass., 94
Bottcher, Herman, 102, 105, 109
Britain, 115
Brooklyn Negro National Congress,
    117
Brooklyn, NY, 117
Browder, Earl, 154
Brown, Archie, 63
Brown, George, 87
Brown Settlement, 15, 18, 30
Brown, Thomas, 158, 176
Brunete, 122, 125, 131-152, 164, 172
Bryan, William Jennings, 103
Bug Club, 71
Bushnell Hospital, 163

Caldwell, Erskine, 133
California, 29
Callion, Walter, 176
Calloway, Cab, 87
Canada, 41, 127
Carney, 147
Cartagena, 116
Carter, Council Gibson, 176
Castillo de San Fernando, 114
Catalan fortress, 114
Champs Elysees, 105-106
Chesterton, 176
Chicago, 15, 23, 29, 32, 38, 40-41, 43-
    59, 63, 65-67, 70, 72-73, 77, 79-80,
    83-87, 94, 117, 119, 126, 137, 143
Chickasawhay River, 15, 20, 30
Chinchon, 120
Chisholm, Albert Edward, 176
Chowan, Mike, 176
Cleveland, Ohio, 127
Cleveland, Roland, 176
Coad, Mack, 176
Cobbs, Walter, 127, 176
Collado, Tomas, 176
Collins, Elijah, 24, 26, 29, 62, 110, 160
Collins, Leroy, 127, 176
Columbia University, 92
Columbus, 144
Columbus, Ohio, 142, 158
Communist Party, 72, 93, 97, 108, 138,
    155

Index

Condor Legion, 115
Congress of Industrial Organizations
(CIO), 76
Corona, Queens, 165
Cotton Club, 89
Covington, Ky., 38-39, 43
Cox, James, 176
The Crisis, 91, 97
Crodowsky, Mr., 52-53, 55-56, 69
Cueria y Orbit, Basilio, 176

Darrow, Clarence, 103
Davis, Angela, 168-69
Dayton, Tenn., 103, 150
Daily Express (London), 145
Delmer, Sefton, 145-48
Democratic National Convention, 97
Depression, 68, 73, 91, 144, 165
Detroit, Mich., 29, 65, 94, 124
Dewey, John, 133
Dicks, Walter, 127, 176
Dickson, Nathaniel, 72-75, 85, 176
Dining Car Employees Union Local
#370, 87
Donawa, Arnold Bennett, 128-29, 176
Du Bois, W.E.B., 83-84, 91
Duclos, Jacques, 155
Dukes, Larry Stratford, 176
Durango, 122

Ebro River, 125, 156-157, 164
Elks, 57
El Escorial, 134-36, 139-41, 171-72
Ellington, Duke, 87
Empire State Building, 82, 89
England, 102, 126, 156
Ethiopia, 91-96, 119, 126, 129, 156
Ethiopian Air Force, 156

Fadiman, Clifton, 133
Father Divine's (restaurant), 86
Federal Bureau of Investigation (FBI),
159, 164
Feingersh, Frank, 155
Fiat, 144
Fighter Squadron 88, 122
Figueras, 114, 156
Finland, 126
Fisher, Dorothy Canfield, 133
Flynn, Errol, 146

Ford, James, 155
Ford Motor Company, 124
For Whom the Bell Tolls, 147
France, 102-104, 107-108, 115, 126,
148, 156, 158-60, 165-66, 172
Franco, 41, 96, 110, 115, 118-19, 133,
147, 156, 158, 166-71, 173
Frankson, Kanute Oliver, 124, 176
Freiheit (song), 134
French Brigade, 120-21, 127
French Trade Union of Paris, 159
Fuentes, 125

Gades, Antonio, 173
Gandesa, 125, 174
Gaffner, 131, 152
Garibaldi Brigade, 131
Garland, Walter Benjamin, 102, 111,
117-20, 150, 170, 176
Garvey, Marcus, 17, 57, 86, 91, 94
Gavin, Eugene Victor, 176
George, Henry, 176
Georgia, 89
Germany, 91, 95, 103, 110, 122
GI Bill, 164
Gibbs, Mr., 24-26
Gibbs, Theodore, 143, 176
Goldwyn, Gerald, 176
Gonne, Maude, 120
Gorky, 112
Graham, Meredith Sydnor, 176
Greenwich Village, 88, 119, 160, 164
Guadalajara, 115, 132-33, 150
Gutierrez, Centurio, 176
Guernica, 122
Gumption, Mr., 25
Gunal, 108, 111

Hampton College, 72
Handy, W. C., 29
Harlem, NY, 48, 82, 86, 88-93, 119,
124, 127-29, 133, 160
Harvard, 56
Harvey, 176
Hendaye, 159
Haywood, Harry, 151, 176
Heidelberg University, 132
Heinkel II and III, 135-36
Hellman, Lillian, 155
Hemingway, Ernest, 126, 145-48, 156

Henry, Belle (aunt), 21-22
Henry, William (uncle), 20-22, 62, 123
Herald Tribune, 107
Herndon, Angelo, 83, 88-89, 127
Herndon, Milton, 127, 158, 176
Hill, T. Arnold, 133
Hitler, 41, 83, 91, 93, 95-96, 115, 119, 122, 132, 165, 171
Hoover, Herbert, 65, 75, 80, 158
Hotel Crillon (Paris), 106
Hotel Grand (NYC), 160
Howard University, 128, 157
Hub, Mr., 22
Hudson River, 99
Hughes, Langston, 84, 112, 150-51
Hunter, John P., 176
Hunter, Oscar Henry, 72, 176

Ibarruri, Delores (La Pasionara), 155, 173
Ile de France, 102
Imes, William Lloyd, 133
International Brigade, 94, 114, 116, 120, 126, 128-29, 141, 151, 156, 158, 164, 171, 173-74
Internationale, The (song), 117
Ireland, 21
Irish Easter Rebellion, 120
Irish Volunteers, 120, 131
Italian Air Force, 156
Italy, 94, 165

Jackson, Burt Edward, 176
James Connolly Column, 120
Jarama, 102, 110, 115-16, 118, 120, 134
Joe, Mr., 22, 24, 56
John, Uncle, 17
Johnson, Aaron Bernard, 176
Johnson, Edward, 127, 158-59
Johnson, Richard, 176
June Bug, 20
Junker, 136

Kansas, 17
Kee, Salaria, 127, 129, 167
Kentucky, 32
Kilpatrick, Admiral, 103-104, 106, 117, 123, 126-27, 131, 155

Ku Klux Klan, 17, 20-22, 27, 32, 88, 118-19
Kurt, 106, 111

L'Arc de Triomphe, 105
Larkin, James, 120
La Guardia, Fiorello, 92
Las Ramblas, 144, 157, 168
Law, Oliver, 72, 75, 85, 102, 119, 126, 129, 137-38, 158, 174
Lawrence, William, 154
Leadbetter, Huddie "Leadbelly", 163
Leadbetter, Martha, 163
League Against War and Fascism, 91, 93
League of Nations, 94
Le Havre, France, 102
Lennon, Gus, 21, 123
Lewis, Abraham, 127, 151, 176
Lewis, Charles, 176
Lewis, Sinclair, 133
Lightfoot, Claude, 72
Lisberg, Norman, 176
Lima, Ohio, 76
Liverpool, 136
London, 92
Londres Hotel, 145
Los Angeles, 94
Louis, Joe, 93
Love, Vaughan, 103-104, 109, 117, 150
Loyalists (Spanish), 113, 115, 127

MacArthur, Douglas, 158
Mackenzie-Papineau Brigade, 131, 137
MacSwiney, Terence, 120
Madison Square Garden, 91
Madison, WI, 66
Madrid, 98, 102, 110, 114-16, 118-22, 132, 134, 137, 139, 141-42, 146, 148, 157, 165, 171, 173-74
Madrid Road, 121
Majorca, 157
Marcantonio, Vito, 92
Marseilles, 166
Marx, Karl, 72, 84
Masons, 57
Mason-Dixon Line, 44, 48, 127
Matthews, Herbert, 145-49
McCarthy era, 164
McDaniels, Eluard Luchell, 150, 176

McGowan, Johnny, 86
McGrotty, John, 120
McKay, Claude, 112
Mediterranean, 114, 158, 166-67
Meridian, Miss., 20, 30, 160, 164
"Miracle of October", 120
Mississippi, 15, 20, 27, 57, 93, 96, 98,
    110, 115, 120, 123, 140, 160, 164
Mississippi River, 27
Mitchell, Andrew, 176
Montille, France, 108
Moody, Frank, 20, 29-63, 77, 110
Mooney, Tom, 98
Moore, William, 176
Morgan, Crawford, 143, 176
Morley, Christopher, 133
Moroccans, 98
Mosca fighter, 136
Mosquito Ridge, 138
Murcia, 154
Muscle Shoals Dam, 29
Mussolini, 83, 92-96, 110, 119, 126,
    129

National Association for the
    Advancement of Colored People
    (NAACP), 91, 97, 164
National Guard, 73-75, 94, 133
National Hunger March of 1932, 158
National Maritime Union, 133
National Negro Congress, 92
National Urban League, 133
Nazi, 95, 106, 118
Nelson, Steve, 138, 166, 174
Newark, NJ, 82
New Jersey, 80, 82
New York City, 15, 23, 77, 79-99, 102,
    104, 106, 117, 129, 159, 163, 166,
    170
New York State, 80
New York Times, 145, 147, 149
Ninety Sixth Division (Spanish
    Division), 164
Normandie, 101
Notre Dame Cathedral, 104

Ohio, 127, 129, 158, 170
Olympics, Berlin, 97
Orange, NJ, 165
O'Reilly, John Joseph, 120

Oriheula, 125, 153, 169
Our Fight, 133
Owens, Jesse, 97

Page, Thomas, 125, 164-65, 176
Palacio de Congresos, 173
Paris, 104-105, 107-108, 159, 165-66,
    168, 172
Parker, Charles Augustus, 145, 176
Parker, Dorothy, 133, 155
Parker, Lizzy (grandmother), 15-16,
    21-22, 154
Peck, James Lincoln Holt, 155-56, 176
Place de la Concorde, 106
Pennsylvania Railroad, 64-65, 75, 85,
    87
Perpignan, 166
Picasso, Pablo, 122
Pilikarpov, 156
Pine Knot, Ky., 34
Pittsburgh, Pa., 76, 87
Plaza Catalonia, 144, 168
Poindexter, 73
Poland, 122, 144
Port Bou, 167
Portugal, 115
Powell, Adam Clayton, 90
Pringle, Claude, 127, 158, 176
Prowell, Alpheus Danforth, 176
Pyrenees, 108-110, 143, 158, 165

Queen Elizabeth, 155
Quitman, Miss., 15, 20-21, 25, 28, 50,
    56, 62-63, 164

Randolph, A. Philip, 76, 92
Ransom, Marcus, 176
RCA Institute, 164
Reed, Arnold, 104
Reeves, Otto, 176
Republican Air Force, 156
Republicans (Spanish Republican
    Govt.), 41, 95, 110, 115-16, 124,
    146, 148, 158, 170, 174
Retiro Park, 173
Rhetta, Virgil, 176
Riejecka, Yugoslavia, 166
Roach, Douglas, 102, 119, 121, 129,
    151
Roberson, James, 72-73, 75, 85, 126

Robeson, Paul, 92, 132, 159, 165
Rochester, Sterling, 119, 177
Rodriguez, Julius, 177
Roosevelt, Franklin D., , 75, 80, 97, 115, 118, 133
Roosevelt, Patrick, 156-57, 163, 165
Rose, Oliver Charles, 177
Rosario, Conrado Figueros, 177
Rucker, Bernard (Barney), 127, 142, 164-65
Rucker, Helen, 165
Russia, 156
Rutgers University, 92
Ryan, Frank, 120-21

San Sebastian, 172
St. Louis, Mo., 29, 158
Savoy Ballroom, 86, 89
Schmeling, Max, 93
Scopes Trial, 103
Scottsboro boys, 98, 117
Seacord, Douglas, 177
Seattle, Wash., 165
Segovia Bridge, 99
Seine River, 104
Selassie, Haile, 94
Shubuta, 20, 23
Sierra del Pandolls, 157
Sixth of February Battalion, Franco-Belgian, 137
Skeeter, Mr., 24-26
Small's Paradise, 86
Smith, Bessie, 29, 48
Smith, "Cotton Ed", 97
Smith, Ferdinand, 133
Spanish Battalion, 121, 137
Spanish People's Army, 116, 122
Socialists, 71
South Carolina, 97
South Pacific, 102
Springfield, Ill., 72-74, 84-85, 110, 126, 133, 137
Stock market crash, 66
Stockyard, 51-52, 64, 69
Stonewall, Miss., 15, 17, 30, 62
Storm Troopers, 41
Strawberry, 20
Sunnyside, Queens, 85, 87
Swanson, Weat, 177
Switzerland, 103

Terragona, 157
Tatum, Mr., 24-25
Taylor, Joseph, 124-25, 177
Tenants Council, 75
Teruel, 145, 147-48, 151, 164
Texas, 57, 126
Thaelmann Brigade, 120, 131, 133-137, 140, 149-52, 158, 171
Thomas, Mr., 52, 55-58
Thompson, Louise, 151
Thornton, Ralph, 151, 177
Trent, Tom, 177
Trettner, Heinz, 122
Truth, Sojourner, 127
Tubman, Harriet, 127
Tupelo, Miss., 60

Underground Railway, 127
Union Square Park, 84-85, 87, 91, 119
Universal Negro Improvement Assoc. (UNIA), 57
University City, 137, 141, 157
University of Chicago, 71
US Army, 72, 102, 163, 165
US Signal Corps, 163
US Supreme Court, 89, 159
Utah, 163

Valencia, 116, 143, 147-48, 152, 156, 169-70, 174
Vallacre, 128
Verdier, Herbert, 177
Victorio, 58
Village Vanguard (NYC), 163
Vallanueva, Pardillo, 174
Volunteer, 156

Wagner Act, 75
Wall (newspaper), 133
Wall Street, 67
Warfield, Frank, 151, 177
Washington, DC, 87, 150, 159
Washington Park (NYC), 71, 83, 85
Waters, George Walter, 177
Watson, Alonzo, 84-85, 88-89, 91, 93-99, 101, 109, 111, 119-22, 129, 158
Weiderman, Jefferson, 177
White, Edward, 102, 111, 177
White House, 158

Wickman, Morris Henry, 150, 177
Wilder, Thornton, 133
Williams, Fred, 177
Williams, Paul E., 155-56, 177
Willis, Sam, 177
Wobblies, 71
Wolfowitz, Herman, 84-85, 88-89, 93-97
Woolworths, 63
World War I, 60, 158
World War II, 102, 163, 165
Works Progress Administration (WPA), 89
Wright, Richard, 72, 85, 133
Wrigleys, 51

Yankees, 16
Yates, Annie (younger sister), 17, 22, 26
Yates, George Washington "Gipson" (father), 17, 21, 23
Yates, Grandfather, 17
Yates, Ida (mother), 15, 22-23, 26, 154
Yates, Idella (older sister), 17, 22, 26
Yates, Louise (daughter), 66
Yates, Richard (son), 70
Youngblood, Charles, 127, 177

Zig, 141